Opportunities and Challenges in the U.S. Labor Market: An Update

Jason Furman
Chairman, Council of Economic Advisers

Recently we have seen noticeable improvement across a broad range of economic indicators. Second-quarter GDP growth rebounded strongly after the negative first quarter. Manufacturing has been particularly strong, with the ISM index reaching its highest level in over three years, and motor vehicle assemblies in the second quarter at the highest rate since 2006. In addition, the Conference Board sentiment index in August reached its highest level of the recovery.

Perhaps no recent economic development has been more surprising than the rapid fall in the unemployment rate and commensurate pickup in the rate of job growth this year. For most of the last several years, the Blue Chip consensus forecast expected the unemployment rate to be around 7 percent right now. As recently as last year, the consensus forecast did not have the annual average unemployment rate falling below 6.1 percent until 2017. As Figure 1 shows, the unemployment rate was 6.1 percent in August—roughly three years ahead of those forecasts.

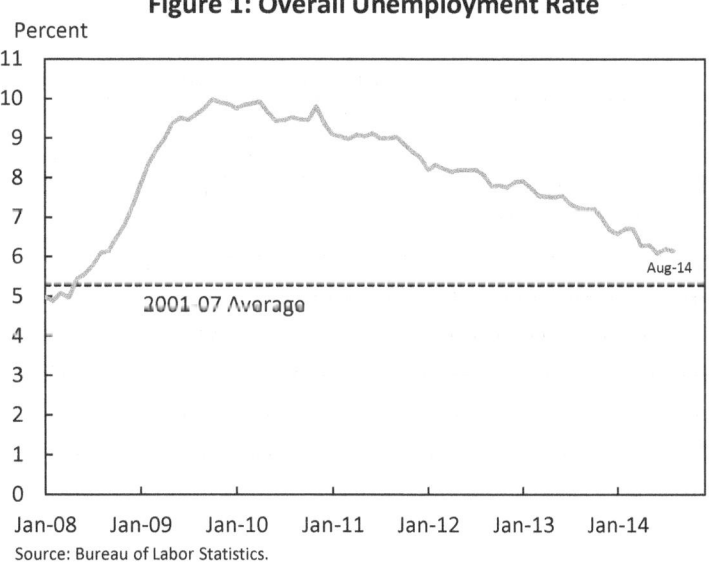

Figure 1: Overall Unemployment Rate

Source: Bureau of Labor Statistics.

But the job market is about more than just the unemployment rate—a successful job market also encourages labor force participation, supports quality jobs, and facilitates effective job matching of workers and positions.

In my remarks today I will discuss the progress we have made in healing from the worst recession since the Great Depression, and also some of the challenges we still face. Some of these challenges are a consequence of the Great Recession, but many of the biggest challenges are longer-standing issues that pre-dated the recession, yet have still affected our ability to recover from it—including long-term unemployment, the number of people working part-time for economic reasons, the participation rate, the decline in labor market churn, and the growth of wages and wage inequality. I will touch on these issues to varying degrees, including going into more depth on the participation rate, drawing on the Council of Economic Advisers' analysis of this topic and, for reasons of space, not doing full justice to the issue of inequality, which I have discussed in more depth elsewhere.[1]

Recent Progress in the Labor Market

In 2009, I remember Larry Summers asking then Treasury Assistant Secretary Alan Krueger about the historical and cross-country experience with labor market recoveries. In 2009, the U.S. unemployment rate had risen much more rapidly than anyone had projected. As recently as November 2008 the Survey of Professional Forecasters projected that the unemployment rate would rise to 7.4 percent in the second quarter of 2009. Instead it rose to 9.3 percent. Larry's question was simple: the unemployment rate can rise rapidly, but how rapidly can it fall?

Alan's answer was sobering. In recent decades, a half dozen OECD countries had seen their unemployment rate rise by more than 4 percentage points in a two-year period. But in these cases, the average annual decline in the unemployment rate in the five years of the recovery was 0.4 percentage point per year and the best case was 0.7 percentage point per year. Moreover, the challenges of growing out of a financial crisis were potentially even more daunting, with Carmen Reinhart and Vincent Reinhart (2010) finding that 10 of 15 countries did not return to pre-crisis levels of unemployment even ten years after their respective crises. This analysis was, unfortunately, prescient for the euro area, which currently has an unemployment rate of 11.5 percent, barely down from its crisis peak of 12.0 percent in 2013.

In part due to the vigorous, multi-front response to the economic crisis, the United States has enjoyed a sustained economic recovery that has exceeded most contemporaneous and historical financial crisis benchmarks.[2] Up until a year ago the unemployment rate was falling by an average of 0.7 percentage point per year, roughly tracking the more recent historical experiences and well exceeding the norm following a financial crisis. In recent months, the pace of the decline in the unemployment rate has increased to over 1 percentage point per year.

---

[1] For a perspective on inequality and the President's agenda see Furman (2014a).
[2] For a discussion of the Recovery Act and other elements of the fiscal response, see Chapter 3 of the Council of Economic Advisers' 2014 Economic Report of the President.

A number of indicators show the recent strengthening in the labor market:

- The participation rate appears to be stabilizing;

- The economy has added 2.5 million jobs in the last year;

- Job growth strengthened over the course of the year, with 215,000 jobs per month so far this year, as compared with the 194,000 jobs per month added during 2013;

- All of the jobs added in the last year are full- time jobs according to the household survey;

- Wage growth has picked up, with average hourly wages (for production and nonsupervisory workers) rising 2.5 percent during the past twelve months, faster than the year-earlier pace and likely continuing to rise somewhat faster than price inflation.

Overall, as Figure 2 shows, these recent months are the continuation of 54 straight months of private-sector job growth—the longest such streak in the Nation's history, and a reflection of the increased consistency of economic performance in recent years compared with the economy in previous decades.[3] Nevertheless, even with this increased consistency, job growth fluctuates from month to month, and there is always a lot of uncertainty, especially about any one data point or any one month.

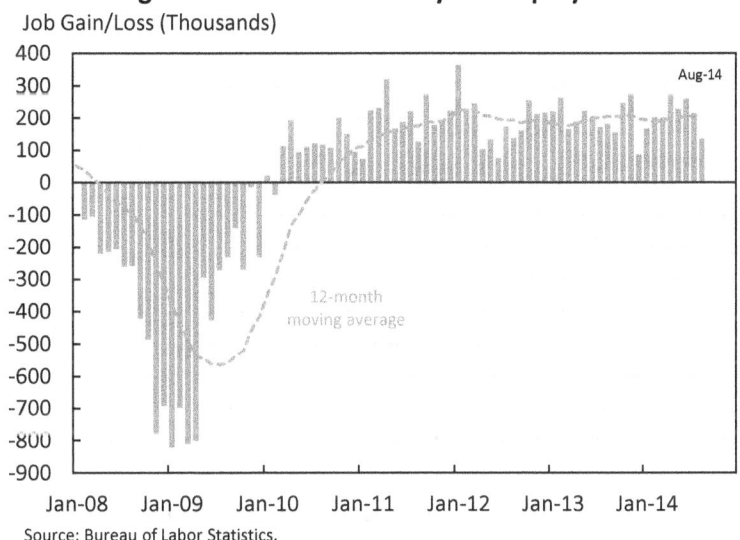

Figure 2: Private Sector Payroll Employment

Source: Bureau of Labor Statistics.

---

[3] For a recent discussion of the "Great Moderation" see Furman (2014b).

The Status of the Labor Market Recovery

A wide range of labor market indicators all tell a consistent story: we are now far into the recovery from the Great Recession—but we are not all the way there yet. The clearest measure of this is the unemployment rate, which rose from 5.3 percent, its average during the 2001-07 expansion period, to peak at 10.0 percent in October 2009. The unemployment rate has since come down to 6.1 percent, which is still unacceptably high but 83 percent of the way back to its pre-recession value—as shown in the first row of Figure 3.

Figure 3: Tracking the Recovery Across Labor Market Indicators
All Data as of August 2014

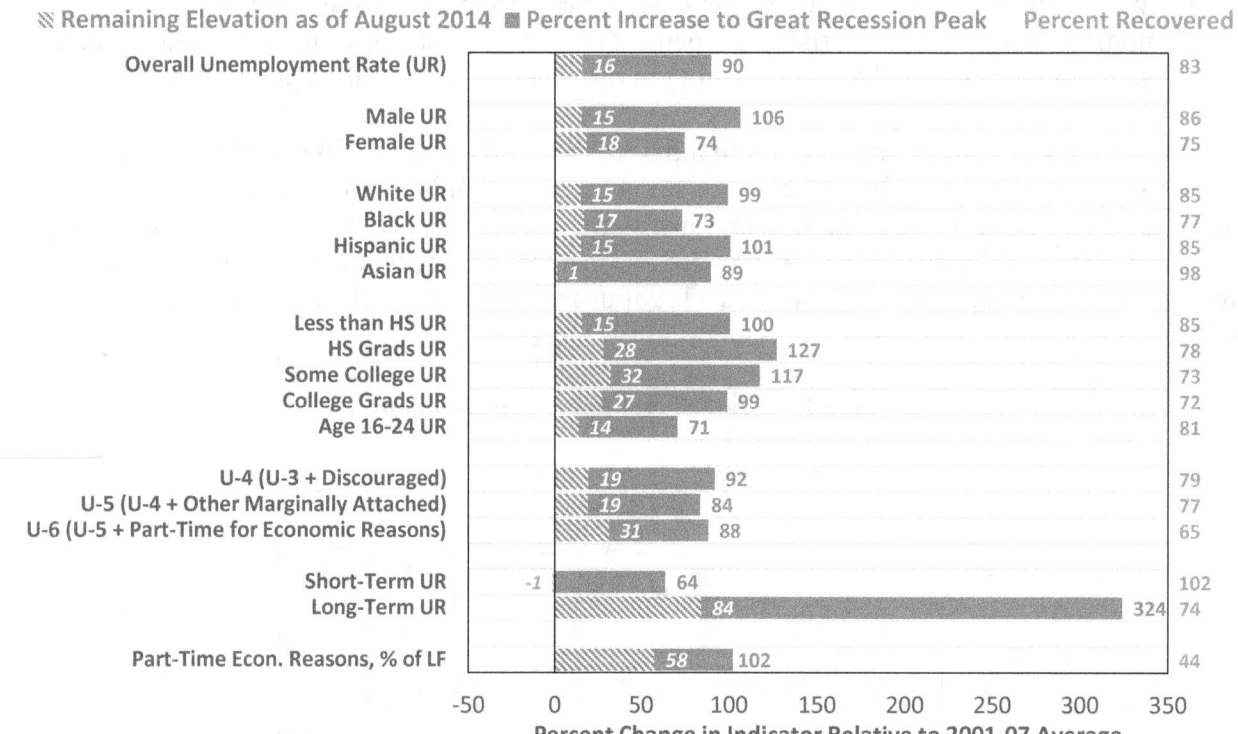

Remaining Elevation as of August 2014 ■ Percent Increase to Great Recession Peak   Percent Recovered

Note: Unemployment rates by education are for persons age 25+. All other rates for persons age 16+ unless noted.
Source: Bureau of Labor Statistics; CEA calculations.

Unemployment by Race, Gender, Age and Education

Figure 3 also shows this recovery metric for a wide range of labor market indicators. Across gender, ethnic and racial groups, unemployment rates rose by about 70 to 110 percent during the recession, and all of these groups have all seen similar magnitudes of recovery—with the current unemployment rates for all these groups at least 75 percent of the way back to their pre-recession levels. Of course, that means that groups with unemployment rates that were already high saw even bigger percentage point increases in their unemployment rates during the recession, and these are precisely the groups that face even larger challenges coping with this enormous setback. Moreover, the fact that the African American unemployment rate, to take one example, is 77 percent of the way back to its pre-recession level is of little comfort when that pre-recession (2001-07) level averaged 9.8 percent. However, research has shown that unemployment disparities were not worsened in this recession and rose in much the same way as in previous recessions (Elsby, Hobijn, and Şahın [2010]).

As is typical with recessions, male unemployment rose more sharply than did women's. In this recession, the large reduction in construction employment contributed to the sharp rise in men's unemployment. While men's unemployment started to recover in 2010, women faced continuing challenges, particularly as State and local government employment began contracting sharply while the private sector started to add jobs. Both men's and women's unemployment continued to recover, however, and today, the unemployment rates for men and women are almost identical.

The extent of recovery is also broadly similar when looking at educational attainment, with the unemployment rates for major categories between 72 and 85 percent of the way back to their pre-recession average. The extent of recovery in the unemployment rate for younger workers aged 16-24 falls squarely within this range—about 81 percent of the way back to pre-crisis levels. But again, this is another instance of a group returning to an already-high rate.[4]

Broader Measures of Unemployment

Other measures of the labor market show the same pattern. For instance, consider the Bureau of Labor Statistics' (BLS) broadest measure of people without jobs—U-5—which includes not only people currently available for work and looking for a job, but also the "marginally attached" who have not looked for a job recently but still report wanting to work. This indicator rose about as much as the official unemployment rate in the recession and is now about 77 percent of the way back to its pre-recession average—meaning that it has recovered just about as much as the official unemployment rate. In the next section I will discuss U-6, an even broader measure that includes not just people without jobs but also people working part-time for economic reasons.

The Structural Challenges in the Labor Market

To point to progress is not to deny the obvious truth that more work remains to be done. The overall unemployment rate is still too high and has not fully recovered—although it is clearly moving in that direction at an increasingly rapid rate. But even if and when the unemployment rate fully recovers to its long-run level, the labor market would still face five interrelated challenges, all of which reflect both trends that pre-date the recession as well as the consequences of the recession, albeit to different degrees. These challenges are the elevation of the long-term unemployment rate, the elevation of involuntary part-time work, the fall in the participation rate, the reduction in labor turnover/dynamism, and the increase in wage inequality. I will briefly discuss four of these issues in this section and then concentrate more fully on the participation rate in the next section.

---

[4] For further discussion on the economic situation for young people, see Furman (2014c).

5

Long-term Unemployment

The short-term unemployment rate, the percentage of the labor force unemployed for 26 weeks or less, is now slightly below its pre-crisis average. But the long-term unemployment rate, the percentage of the labor force unemployed for 27 weeks or longer, remains elevated. In the recession, the long-term unemployment rate more than quadrupled, as opposed to the short-term unemployment rate which increased 64 percent. However, over the past year we have seen notable progress in reducing long-term unemployment. In particular, looking over the last 12 months, declining long-term unemployment accounts for about three-quarters of the drop in the overall unemployment rate (Figure 4). This is a disproportionate share given that about one-third of the jobless are long-term unemployed. And crucially, this decline in long-term unemployment coincides with a stabilization in the participation rate, and with a pick-up in job-finding rates for the long-term unemployed (Cajner and Ratner [2014]), suggesting that the headline figures we are seeing are genuinely good news.[5]

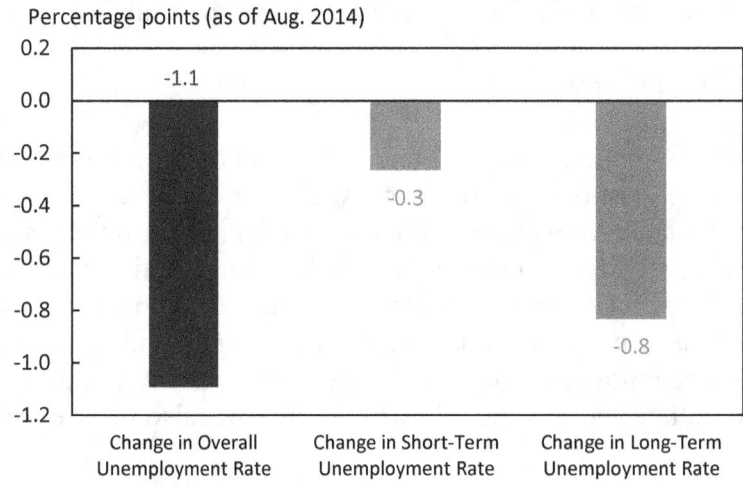

Figure 4: 12-Month Change in Unemployment Rate
Percentage points (as of Aug. 2014)

Note: Based on percent distribution of unemployed reported in table A-12.
Source: Bureau of Labor Statistics; CEA calculations.

Moreover, the remaining cyclical challenge of long-term unemployment is well within our power to solve. The evidence shows that while the long-term unemployed have very similar characteristics to the short-term unemployed, a spell of bad luck can become prolonged and extraordinary hardship, especially if employers become averse to giving these workers a chance (Krueger, Cramer, and Cho [2014] and Ghayad [2014]). In addition, research has found that the current period of elevated long-term unemployment does not appear to be a result of compositional shifts in demographics, occupations, industries, regions, or reasons for unemployment (Kroft et al. [2014]). This suggests that there are not structural impediments to further declines in the long-term unemployment rate, and this gives us hope that steps we take to further the recovery should be able to address the challenge.

---

[5] Cajner and Ratner (2014) note that the recent rise in job finding rates is apparent for one-year unemployment-to-employment flows, but less apparent for month-to month changes.

Still, even after the near-term cyclical challenge of long-term unemployment is addressed, there will be important questions about why it soared to unprecedented levels in the recession. To answer this question, I believe we will have to look not just at the massive shock that hit the economy, but at the evolving nature of U.S. business cycles. Figure 5 shows the fraction of the total increase in the unemployment rate attributable to long-term unemployment for 10 business cycles going back to 1948. This fraction has clearly grown over time, and had been increasing even prior to 2007.

Figure 5: Increase in Long-Term Unemployment as a Percent of Increase in Overall Unemployment Rate

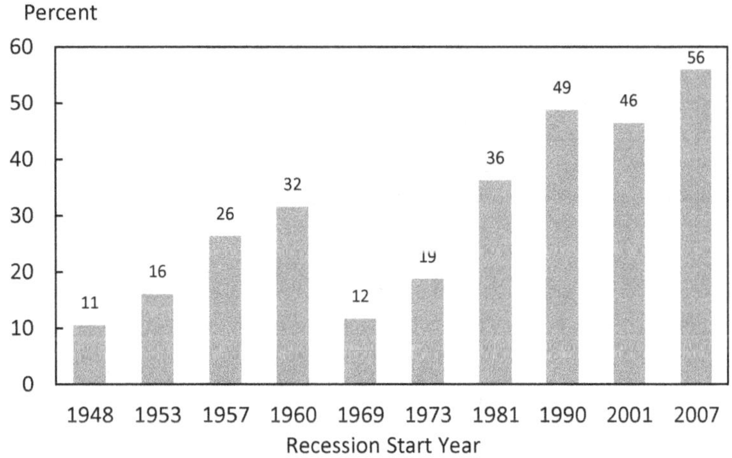

Percent

Recession Start Year	Percent
1948	11
1953	16
1957	26
1960	32
1969	12
1973	19
1981	36
1990	49
2001	46
2007	56

Source: Bureau of Labor Statistics; CEA calculations.

Not only has long-term unemployment become more cyclically sensitive than it was in the past, but at least during the 2001-2007 expansion, the fraction of the jobless that were long-term unemployed remained noticeably higher than in past expansions, even as the recovery unfolded. Figure 6 plots long-term unemployment as a percent of total unemployment, and the green line connects the local minima during business-cycle expansion periods. Over the 1970s, 1980s, and 1990s, the trough in long-term unemployment edged up from about 5 percent to about 10 percent of total unemployment. And following the early 2000s recession, it never returned below about 16 percent. Thus, while we continue to see substantial scope for reducing long-term unemployment, the experience during the 2000s creates an open question about precisely what the steady-state rate of long-term unemployment is.

7

Figure 6: Long-Term Unemployment as a Percent of Total

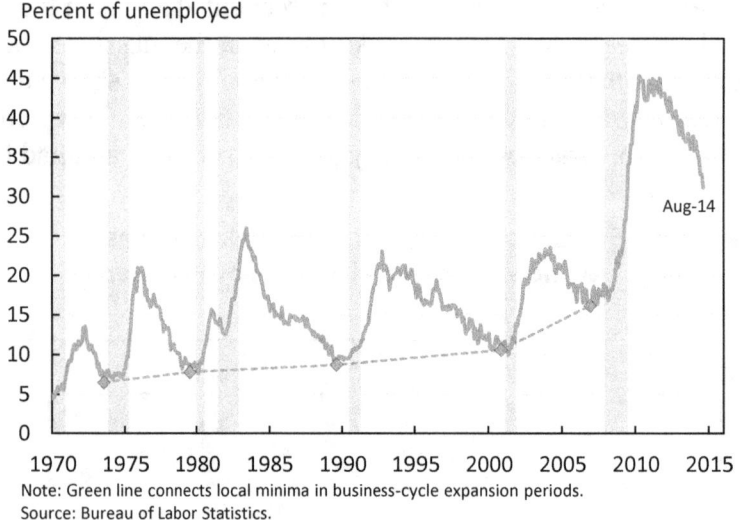

Percent of unemployed

Note: Green line connects local minima in business-cycle expansion periods.
Source: Bureau of Labor Statistics.

One potential explanation for this set of observations is reduced labor market churn, a topic I will discuss soon. For now, let me just say that reduced churn may mean that those who experience the misfortune of job loss get stuck in that position for longer periods. And if this is the case, it means that the pain of recessions are becoming even more acutely concentrated, which has major implications for thinking about countercyclical stabilization policy.

Part-Time for Economic Reasons

An even more expansive measure of labor underutilization than the official unemployment rate is the U-6 rate, which includes the people without jobs covered in the U-5 and also people working part-time hours for economic reasons (i.e., involuntarily). The U-6 rate has also come down steadily, falling by more than 5 percentage points from its peak of 17.2 percent in early 2010, but it still remains about 3 percentage points above its pre-crisis rate, indicating a smaller recovery relative to its original base. It is worth noting, however, that average weekly hours for production and non-supervisory workers as measured in the establishment survey, sends a different signal—showing an almost complete recovery from the recession.

The main reason for this additional elevation in the U-6 is people working part-time for economic reasons, a group which grew dramatically in the recession and, while it has declined substantially since 2010, still remains elevated. In the recovery, 95 percent of the jobs added have been full time, and that number is over 100 percent in the last year. Moreover, as shown in Figure 7, the decline in the number of persons working part-time for economic reasons has followed a pattern similar to previous recoveries, but not enough to offset the initial massive rise in involuntary part-time work. The severity of the Great Recession may have played a role in influencing patterns of part-time work during this business cycle.

Figure 7: Part-Time for Economic Reasons During Recoveries

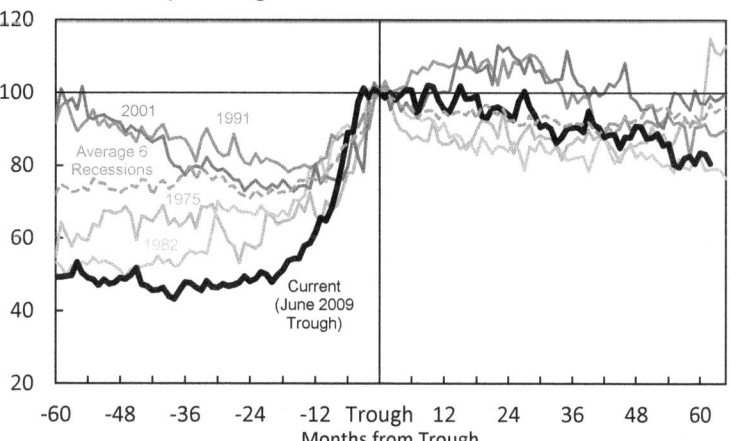

Note: Data have been adjusted for the 1994 CPS redesign following Polivka and Miller (1998).
Source: Bureau of Labor Statistics; CEA calculations.

Labor Market Flows

Beyond unemployment measures, it is instructive to look at labor market flows. Flows are relevant to the recovery because they reflect, in part, the ability of workers to make changes to improve their employment situation and status. The flow out of unemployment following a recession is of obvious concern, but other flows can also inform our view of the recovery.

The picture here also shows substantial recovery (Figure 8). Consistent with the strong employment growth over the last 54 months, the rate of new job openings (as a share of total positions) is now above its pre-recession average after falling by almost 50 percent during the recession. Layoffs and discharges are below their pre-recession level after seeing a substantial uptick in the recession. The rate of new hires has also regained more than half its recessionary decline and is now approaching its pre-recession level. The quit rate has followed a similar pattern to the hires rate and has also recovered more than half of its decline. This is particularly reassuring because it tells us that workers are moving on to better employment opportunities at substantially higher rates that during the crisis. Taken together, the flows data indicate that the labor market is moving again.

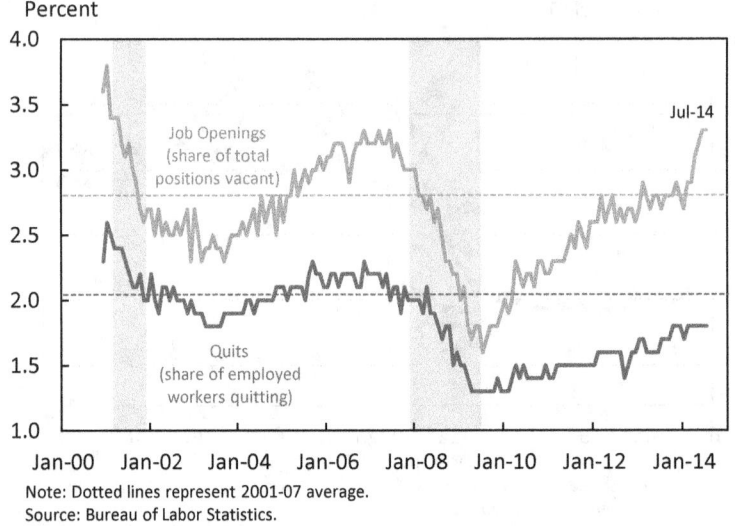

Figure 8: Job Opening and Quit Rates

Note: Dotted lines represent 2001-07 average.
Source: Bureau of Labor Statistics.

But while the near-term trend is towards increasing dynamism, the longer-run picture is not as reassuring. Over the decades preceding the Great Recession, a wide range of measures of dynamism declined. This is true at the level of individual workers: fewer workers change employers, change occupations or move across State or county lines, some of which can be seen in Figures 9 and 10 below. We also see a similar phenomenon at the business level, both with fewer new jobs or businesses being created, but at the same time fewer old jobs or businesses being destroyed or failing, some of which is shown in Figure 11 below. Moreover, we have seen a divergence in growth in establishments and new firms, as growth at the establishment level has stabilized while growth in new firm entry has continued to decline.

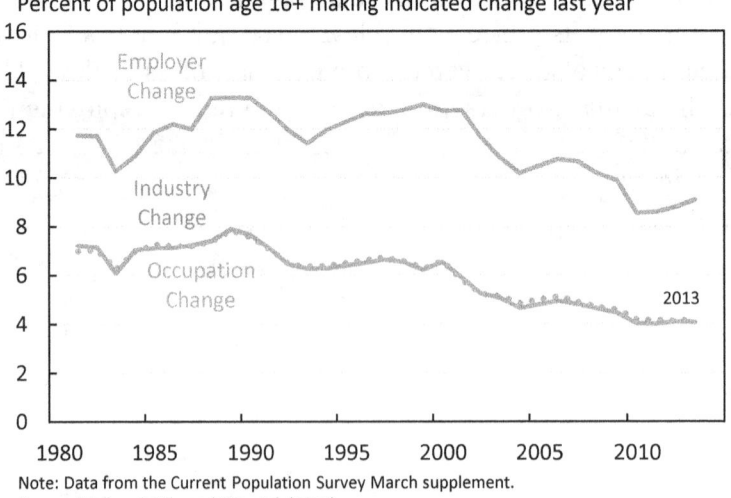

Figure 9: Employer, Occupation and Industry Transitions

Note: Data from the Current Population Survey March supplement.
Source: Molloy, Smith, and Wozniak (2014).

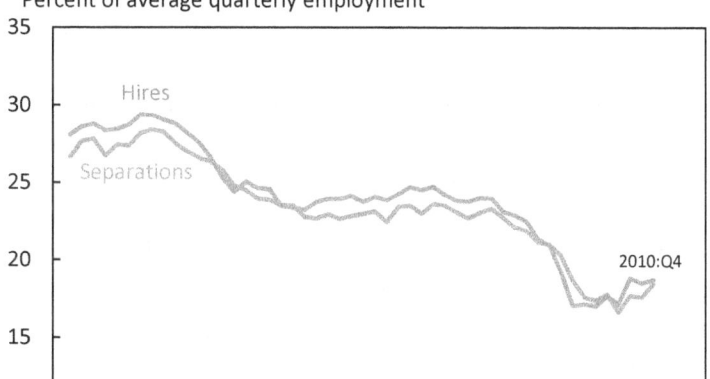

Figure 10: Trends in Hires and Separations

Percent of average quarterly employment

Note: Data from the Longitudinal Employer-Household Dynamics program.
Source: Hyatt and Spletzer (2013).

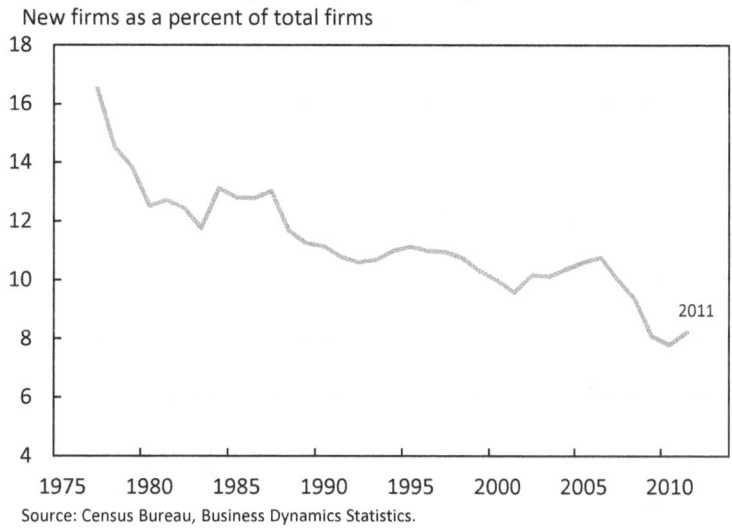

Figure 11: Firm Entry Rate

New firms as a percent of total firms

Source: Census Bureau, Business Dynamics Statistics.

These changes are puzzling because there is no evidence that the economy itself is subject to fewer shocks. If anything, some have pointed to evidence from the manufacturing sector to argue that there are more industry-level productivity shocks, as some areas do much better and others do worse. Also, the shift of the economy away from manufacturing and union jobs and towards service sector and non-union jobs would be expected to increase turnover.

Some of the other possible hypotheses may explain portions of the data, but fail to explain the broad overarching trend. For instance, these changes are not related to housing prices or the aging of the population. They also cut across wide groups and are not confined to particular groups, like dual-income married couples. It is most likely that many factors are driving a structural change, and we are working to figure out what they are.

It is, of course, unclear how we should react to changes in labor market turnover, and economists are divided on this question. In contrast to wages and employment, we have no direct interest in

11

encouraging churn per se. In some respects reduced churn has benefits, like more stable jobs with less disruption for workers and more stable matches with ability to grow job-specific human capital for employers.

Moreover, some of the explanations for reduced churn suggest that there may not be a public policy failure that needs correcting. Long-term trends toward lower churn could reflect an improvement in employers' ability to hire workers that are well matched for their jobs, leading to longer-term employment. Alternatively, broader forces that are increasing returns to human capital could be increasing the value of job-specific knowledge and experience, reducing the optimal frequency of job transitions. Similarly, the shift from small stores to large retailers, for example, could both result in improvements for consumers in the form of lower prices and better selection as well as more job stability and room for internal promotion for employees.

Nevertheless, there are a number of reasons to be concerned about declining turnover, both as a symptom of other issues and also as a cause of them in its own right. Some of the concerns are: (1) reduced turnover leading to lower overall employment rates and higher long-term unemployment due to a less fluid labor market (Davis and Haltiwanger [2014]); (2) smaller wage gains and potentially increased inequality as people have less ability to move to jobs that pay higher wages and less leverage to bargain with their current employers; and (3) lower productivity growth as capital and labor are reallocated less quickly and efficiently to their most productive uses.

Clearly, this is an area where we need to improve our understanding of the causes and consequences of reduced turnover, and their implications for public policy.

Wages

Real wage growth has been relatively stagnant for several decades leading up to the Great Recession, in part because of slower productivity growth and in part because the benefits of that productivity growth have disproportionately gone to households at the top of the income distribution. As a result, household income gains in the 1980s and 1990s were primarily generated by the increase in female labor force participation—and so, as the growth in female labor force participation stalled after 1999, so did those household income gains.

Real average hourly earnings (for production and nonsupervisory workers) rose in the Great Recession as the price level fell, but then a combination of declining nominal wage growth and inflation moved real wages in the other direction in the first years of the recovery. As shown in Figure 12, however, as labor markets have strengthened nominal wage growth has picked up— and for the last year and a half wage growth has exceeded inflation, although it still falls well below productivity growth and well below the levels needed to make up for decades of stagnation. And although it is outside the scope of my remarks today, there is substantial evidence to suggest that we should be concerned about the distribution of wage growth underlying this average.

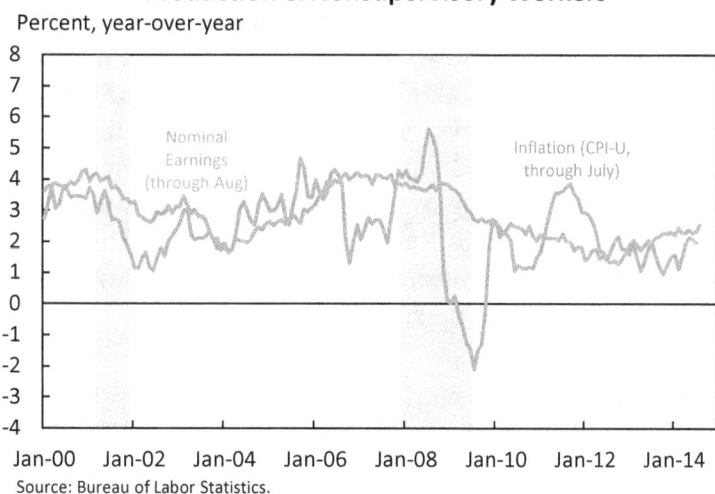

Figure 12: Average Hourly Earnings for Private Production & Nonsupervisory Workers

Percent, year-over-year

Nominal Earnings (through Aug)

Inflation (CPI-U, through July)

Source: Bureau of Labor Statistics.

The Evolution of the Participation Rate

You may notice one indicator that was not included in Figure 3 on the labor market recovery: the participation rate. While the unemployment rate and a range of other indicators are coming down and are on track to return to pre-crisis rates, the participation rate is a different story. As is widely known, it has fallen over the course of the recovery, although it appears to have stabilized since last October, during which time the unemployment rate has come down sharply.

However, unlike the unemployment rate and the other indicators in Figure 3, we should not expect the participation rate to return to its pre-crisis levels and in fact, we were not expecting that prior to the crisis.

To see this, consider what would have happened if you had asked someone in 2006 to forecast the unemployment rate for 2014. They would have started from an average of the previous years and would have thought that such an average would yield a reasonable forecast for the future. However, if you had asked the same person to forecast the participation rate, they would not have assumed that the recent historical average was a particularly good guide. Instead they would have noted that the first baby boomers (born in 1946) would turn age 62 in 2008 and become eligible for Social Security and that a steady decline in the participation rate would follow.

In other words, a decline in the participation rate was predictable and it was predicted. The 2004 *Economic Report of the President* predicted that the participation rate would decline about half a percentage point by the end of 2009 but stated "the decline may be greater, however, after 2008, which is the year that the first baby boomers... reach the early retirement age of 62."

Someone in 2006 might also have noted that on top of this age-related trend, the participation rate for prime-age men, those age 25 to 54, had fallen nearly continuously since 1953, as shown in Figure 13A.[6] They would also have noted that a several decade long increase in women's labor force participation stalled and started to reverse, with the 2006 the participation rate for prime age women falling slightly below its value from a decade earlier despite a reduction in the unemployment rate over that period, as shown in Figure 13B. In fact, a 2006 paper by five Federal Reserve economists (Aaronson et al. [2006]) who are some of the leading analysts of these issues predicted that due to a combination of aging effects and the non-aging trends we had seen, the participation rate would fall to 62.9 percent in 2014—almost exactly what it is right now. I do not point out this number to suggest that I think the study was exactly right—the authors certainly did not factor in the Great Recession and additional analysis, including subsequent work by those authors, sheds further light on these issues. But the 2006 study does put the decline in the participation rate in perspective.

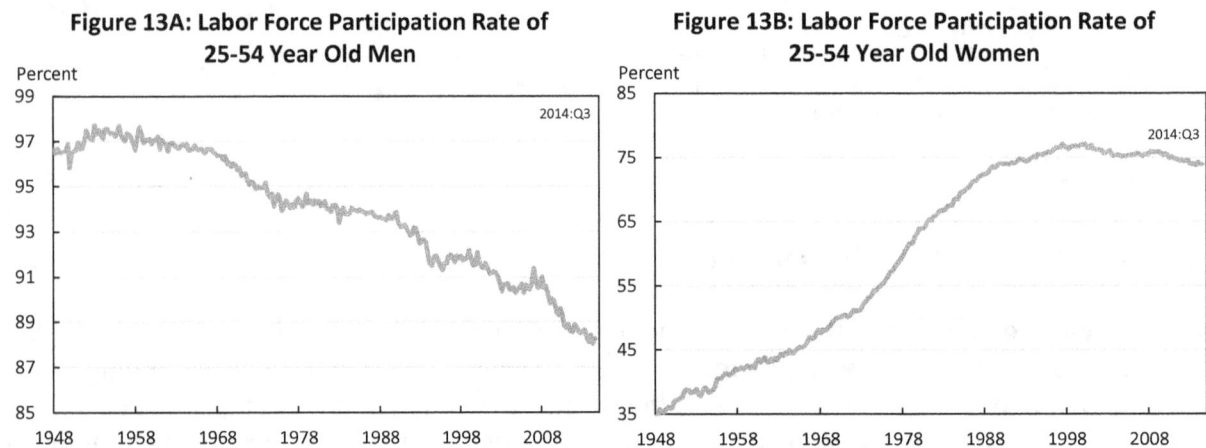

Figure 13A: Labor Force Participation Rate of 25-54 Year Old Men

Source: Bureau of Labor Statistics.

Figure 13B: Labor Force Participation Rate of 25-54 Year Old Women

Source: Bureau of Labor Statistics.

A recent Council of Economic Advisers study analyzed the causes of the decline in the participation rate, what it means for different groups, and the outlook for the participation rate and the implications for policy. The overall analysis is generally in the middle of the range of estimates from over a half dozen other studies of the topic. I will briefly summarize some of the conclusions and the analysis that led us to those conclusions.

The Causes of the Decline in the Participation Rate

From 2007-Q4 to 2014-Q3 the participation rate fell by 3.1 percentage points. Our report decomposed this reduction in the participation rate into three factors:

- <u>We estimate that the aging of the population is responsible for 1.7 percentage points of the decline in the participation rate, slightly more than half of the total decline.</u> Because older individuals participate in the labor force at lower rates than younger workers, the aging of the population that is shown in Figure 14 exerts downward pressure on the overall labor force participation rate. While older workers today are participating in the labor force at higher rates than older workers of previous generations, these changes are tiny compared to the very large drop-off in participation when workers enter their early

---

[6] For data in this section, 2014:Q3 is the average of reported figures for July and August.

60s.[7] To estimate this aging trend we held participation rates constant at their 2007 levels and allowed the demography to vary.[8] Our estimate that about half of the decline in the participation rate is driven by the aging of the population is consistent with estimates by the Congressional Budget Office (CBO [2014]) and roughly in the middle of the range from a range of other studies.[9] This part of the decline in the participation rate is unrelated to the Great Recession and, although it may be offset by other policies, should not be expected to reverse as the economy improves.

Figure 14: Share of the Adult Population Over Age 55

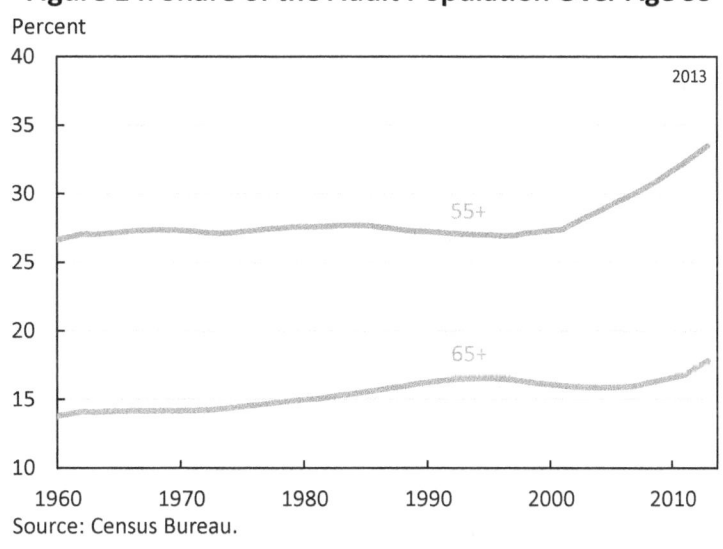

Source: Census Bureau.

- Typical business-cycle effects are currently responsible for an estimated 0.4 percentage point of the decline in the participation rate, about one-seventh of the overall decline. Elevation in the unemployment rate typically means a decline in labor force participation, as potential workers defer looking for a job until the economy improves. Time series analysis of historical data shows that each 1 percentage point increase in the unemployment rate is responsible for a 0.2 percentage point reduction in the participation rate, as shown in Figure 15. So as the unemployment rate comes down the participation rate should improve, and the evidence suggests that when the unemployment rate has fully recovered, the increased labor demand will also bring roughly another 1 million workers back into the labor force over time.

---

[7] To put this in context, the participation rate for workers age 55 and over has risen from 38.8 percent in 2007-Q4 to 40.1 percent in 2014-Q3. But aging has still driven down the overall participation rate because both of these numbers are well below the 81.0 percent average for ages 25 to 54—and thus shifting a higher share into older age groups dwarfs any change within the older group, driving down the overall participation rate.

[8] Note, our method relies on using participation rates for single-year age groups. Some analysis using 10 year groups misses significant shifts within the 55-64 year old age group and thus understate the aging trend. Our estimate of the aging trend is slightly smaller if you fix participation rates at their 2014 levels and project back with the changed demography, since the Great Recession has slightly narrowed the gap in participation between prime-age and older individuals.

[9] For a comparison to other estimates see Table 1 of CEA (2014).

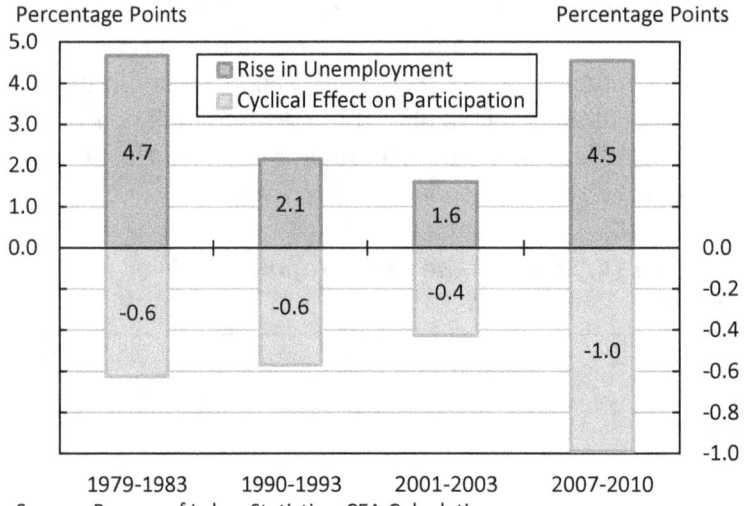

Figure 15: Cyclical Declines In Labor Force Participation

Source: Bureau of Labor Statistics; CEA Calculations.

- The remaining 1.0 percentage point of the decline in the participation rate, or one-third of the total decline since the end of 2007, is not fully understood. In our econometric analysis we find that this portion is not explained by either the aging of the population or the current recession. One possibility that could explain part of this decline is a continuation of the pre-recession trends of declining participation rates conditional on age for many cohorts, for example the over six-decade long decline in prime-age male labor force participation. Another possibility that likely also explains at least a portion of this decline is the very severe recession, with its unique characteristics leading to a greater than average decline in participation. For example, we find that we attribute more of the decline in participation to cyclical factors if we control separately for long-term unemployment. To the degree that this unexplained decline is related to the Great Recession, then recovery should bring back even more than the roughly 1 million people associated with the conventional cyclical effect. Additionally, there are structural changes in the labor market—such as the decline in labor market flows—that may have exacerbated the decline in participation for a given rise in unemployment. This is clearly an area that warrants more study. Further, while we did look for evidence of an unusual role for disability insurance or school enrollments, we found that both have had a standard cyclical effect on the participation rate in the recession and current recovery— and if anything disability insurance has grown less than we would have expected, as shown in Figure 16.

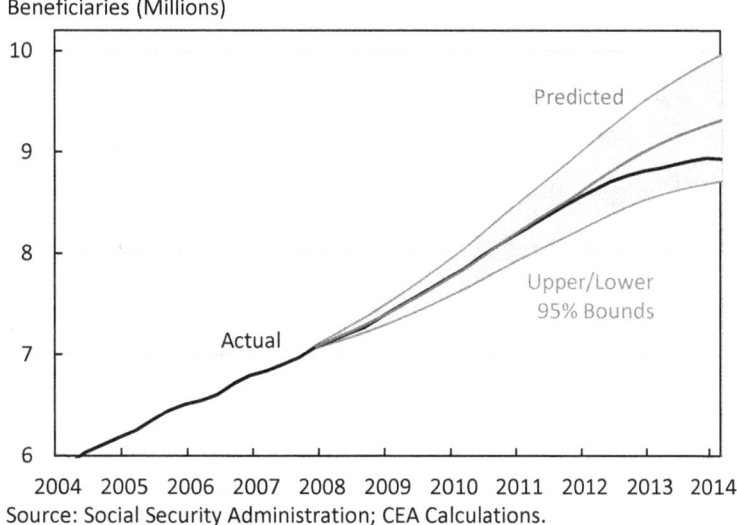

Figure 16: Predicted SSDI Beneficiaries

Beneficiaries (Millions)

Source: Social Security Administration; CEA Calculations.

The evolution of these three factors over the course of the recovery are shown in Figure 17, with the demographic trend consistently growing more negative while the cyclical effects have waxed and waned and the residual has grown. In fact, from the beginning of 2011 to the third quarter of 2014, looking just at the last three and a half years, the participation rate fell by 1.3 percentage points. Nearly 80 percent of that decline (1.0 percentage point) can be directly attributed to the aging of the population and increased retirements.

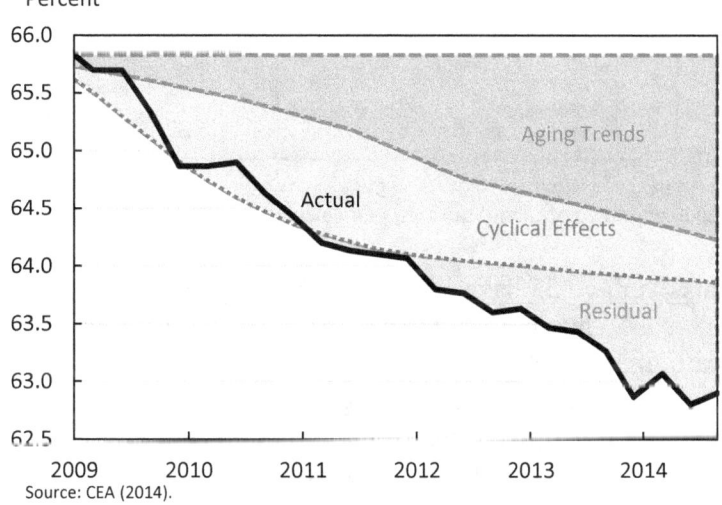

Figure 17: Labor Force Participation Decomposition

Percent

Source: CEA (2014).

Our report included an in depth discussion of the trends in participation rates for a number of groups, let me briefly highlight a few of them:

- <u>Young people ages 16 to 24 have seen a steady decline in their participation rate for several decades—although this entirely reflects changing schooling and work choices.</u> Since 1980, the participation rate for young people has fallen by about 15 percentage points. Between 1980 and the mid-1990s, most of this decline was due to increasing enrollment in school, but since the mid-1990s the reduction in participation is largely due to fewer students working while simultaneously enrolled in school. Over the last two decades, the share of 16-24 year olds neither enrolled in school nor participating in the labor force has neither risen nor decreased as shown in Figure 18, suggesting that changes in schooling behavior account for all of the decrease in the youth participation rate.

Figure 18: Labor Force Participation Rate of 16-24 Year Olds

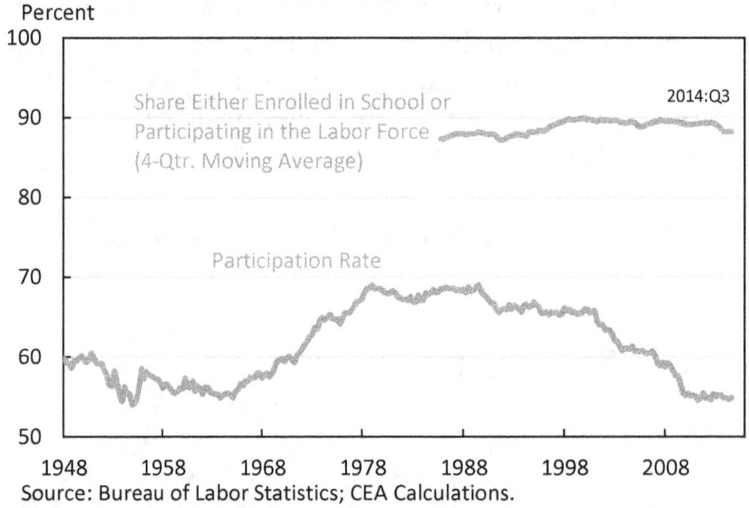

Percent

Source: Bureau of Labor Statistics; CEA Calculations.

- <u>Older individuals over age 55 have steadily increased their participation over the last two decades</u>. This increase, shown in Figure 19, has reversed what had been a decades-long decline in the participation rate for this group. Rising educational attainment, increased labor force participation of wives, and changes in Social Security have been identified as factors responsible for this upward trend. Participation also likely rose due to improvements in health and workplace technology.

Figure 19: Labor Force Participation Rate of Individuals 55 and Older

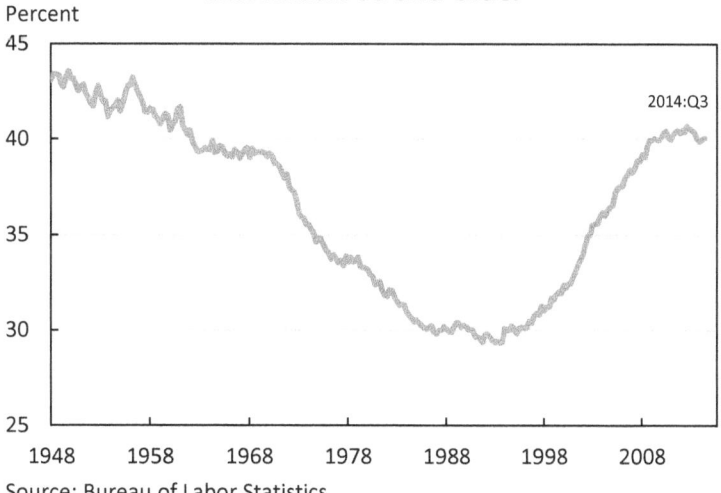

Source: Bureau of Labor Statistics.

- Prime-age women (ages 25 to 54) increased their participation rapidly from 1970 through 2000, before participation for this group declined slightly over the past decade. A number of factors came together to produce the rapid raise in women's participation—declining discrimination and increasing legal protection against discrimination, widespread availability of more effective birth control in the form of the pill, greater equality in all aspects of education, and changes in economic forces stemming from the increased education of women, the advent of labor-saving household technology and greater international trade. As these forces tapered in the 1990s, additional incentives arose such as the expansion of the Earned Income Tax Credit (EITC); and the replacement of Aid to Families with Dependent Children (AFDC) with the work-centered Temporary Assistance to Needy Families (TANF); and reforms to divorce laws. However, the United States remains without many of the types of programs implemented in other countries to support working families and bolster female participation, such as paid leave and affordable childcare. Partly as a result, in recent years the United States has gone from a leader among developed economies in female participation to falling behind many of our peers, as shown in Figure 20.

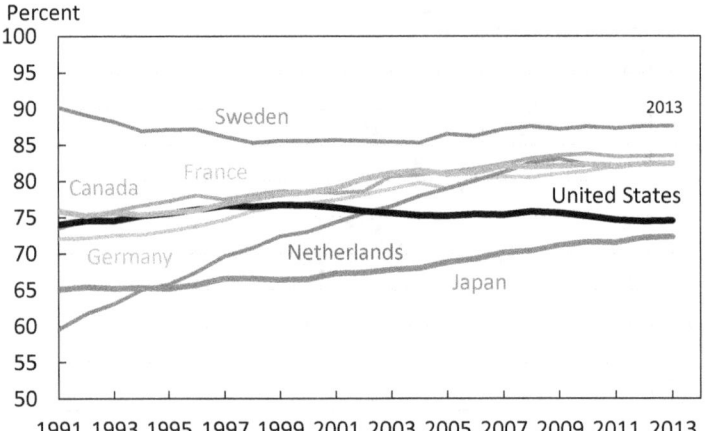

Figure 20: Labor Force Participation Rate of 25–54 Year Old Women

Note: Workers on leave are included in the labor force.
Source: International Labor Organization.

- <u>Men have experienced a substantial decline in labor force participation and employment over the last sixty years.</u> In 1950, 92 percent of prime-age men were employed, but that figure has fallen to 83 percent—the result of a steady decline in participation in the labor force for over sixty years. Prime-age black men have an even lower employment-to-population ratio, at 73 percent, and a large gap persists between the employment-population ratio for white men and black men.

Table 1 - Male Labor Market Indicators, 1950 vs. 2014:Q2

	Participation Rate		Unemployment Rate		Employment-Population Ratio		Share Either Enrolled or Participating	
	1950	2014:Q2	1950	2014:Q2	1950	2014:Q2	1950	2014:Q2
Prime-Age Men	94.7	88.0	3.4	5.3	91.5	83.4	--	--
Prime-Age White Men	95.1	89.4	3.1	4.4	92.1	85.5	--	--
Prime-Age Black Men	92.0	80.4	6.0	9.5	86.4	72.8	--	--
Prime-Age Hispanic Men	92.9	90.7	8.0	5.3	85.5	85.9	--	--
Young Men	68.2	56.0	7.0	14.4	63.4	48.0	77.2	89.7
Young White Men	67.9	59.1	6.8	12.5	63.3	51.7	77.2	90.6
Young Black Men	71.7	49.8	9.1	24.9	65.2	37.3	77.0	84.6
Young Hispanic Men	70.4	56.0	13.0	13.5	61.2	48.5	76.2	90.3

Sources: 1950 Census 1% Sample; Bureau of Labor Statistics; CEA calculations.

- <u>Black male participation has been declining more rapidly than the white male participation rate since the mid-1970s and that there is a larger racial gap in employment and unemployment today.</u> In 1950 the participation rate for black men was slightly below that of white men, but by 2014 the gap had widened substantially. The decline in participation has been particularly extreme among young black men and black men with lower education levels as young black male participation has fallen almost in half from where it was in 1950. A similar gap has opened up in the broader category of "in school or employed." This has been caused by the evolution of the economy and job market opportunities, as well as the sharp rise in incarceration of young black men, since discrimination against those who were previously incarcerated reduces labor market opportunities even after sentences are completed.

The Outlook for the Participation Rate

This diagnosis of the causes of the decline in the participation rate helps to inform our understanding of its evolution in the coming years. The aging trend will continue to push the participation rate down by about 0.2 percentage point per year. As the economy continues its recovery, the cyclical component of the decline in the participation rate should disappear—adding 0.5 percentage point to the participation rate spread over a number of years, although the exact period for this effect is difficult to predict. The portion of the decline in the participation rate due to unexplained factors is even more difficult to predict. To the degree it is the result of non-aging trends, then a continuation of them could further lower the participation rate. Alternatively, to the degree this unexplained component is a consequence of the Great Recession then as the economy continues its healing this effect could disappear, putting upward pressure on the participation rate over a number of years. As shown in Figure 21, our analysis suggests the non-aging, non-cyclical component of the decline in labor force participation is substantial. For this and the other obvious reasons, the participation trend deserves careful monitoring.

Absent changes in policies, a meaningful increase in the participation rate from current rates appears unlikely. Figure 21 shows several scenarios for the participation rate with a common assumption about the aging trend but varying assumptions about the evolution of the cyclical and residual components. These scenarios are not projections and do not represent the full range of possibilities, but they do indicate that the participation rate is likely to be roughly stable in the near term and will decrease more rapidly after the economy returns to full employment and the effects of population aging once again dominate.

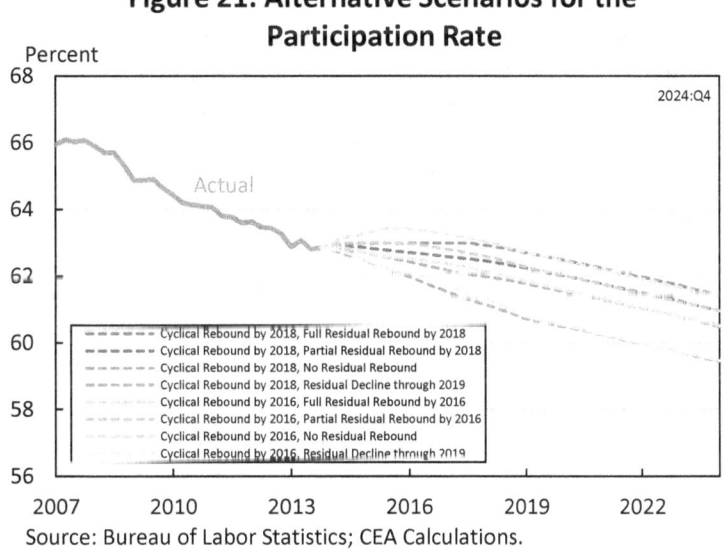

Figure 21: Alternative Scenarios for the Participation Rate

Source: Bureau of Labor Statistics; CEA Calculations.

The Agenda for a Stronger Labor Market Going Forward

I have discussed five interrelated challenges that have been building since before the Great Recession and will continue to face the economy after we have recovered: long-term unemployment, involuntary part-time work, labor force participation, labor force and business churn, and real wage growth. The President has put forward a robust agenda to address these interrelated issues.

I want to outline four major areas of policy informed by this discussion:

First, strengthen the economic recovery, especially for the long-term unemployed

We have made a lot of progress in lowering the unemployment rate but at 6.1 percent it is still unacceptably high. Moreover, the participation rate is below what it would be at full employment. Continuing to speed the economy's return to full employment will require additional aggregate demand and other steps to enhance jobs and growth.

The President has proposed a $302 billion, multi-year surface transportation reauthorization plan. We know from a large body of economic research that sound infrastructure investments boost long-term economic growth and productivity. We also know that maintaining assets in a good state of repair is one of the best investments we can make (Kahn and Levinson [2011]).

The President's plan would put a down payment on addressing major infrastructure gaps in this country. It would prioritize "fix-it-first" investments to improve the safety and efficiency of highways, bridges, and transit systems while also supporting thousands of jobs in the construction sector, which was particularly hard hit in the recession and which continues to exhibit elevated unemployment today.

The President's Budget also proposed to increase investments in research, education, security, and other critical areas through an Opportunity, Growth, and Security Initiative. This proposal would both speed the return to full employment and help lay the groundwork for stronger long-run growth, reducing the cyclical component of the participation rate.

Housing is a particularly important area for the macroeconomy. Mortgage credit is currently tighter than other forms of credit, and one reason that lenders point to is uncertainty over the conditions under which Fannie Mae, Freddie Mac and the Federal Housing Agency (FHA) will obligate lenders to repurchase mortgages that would otherwise be guaranteed or insured—which has been called "put-back risk." In May, the FHA embarked on a program to address these concerns, and acting independently, Federal Housing Finance Administration (FHFA) Director Mel Watt has also undertaken steps to provide clarity on put-back risk and thereby ease credit constraints in the mortgage market. Also, the Administration has extended the Making Home Affordable program to continue to help struggling homeowners facing foreclosure or whose mortgages are underwater.

Other steps would help growth and job creation, like reauthorizing the Export-Import Bank. In the absence of action from Congress, President Obama will press forward by using his executive authority to speed the permitting of infrastructure projects, launch new hubs of manufacturing innovation and attract foreign investment.

All of these measures would help lower the overall unemployment rate which, as we have seen, is the best way to lower the long-term unemployment rate. But we should not overlook some of the unique challenges the long-term unemployed can face. That is why it disappointing that Congress has failed to extend the Emergency Unemployment Compensation (EUC) program, which would also boost economic activity and aggregate demand by supporting job-seekers' incomes while they are unemployed. Moreover, research shows that EUC helps long-term unemployed workers stay connected to the labor force and keep looking for work.

In addition, earlier this year the President convened private sector leaders to discuss how the government and private industry can work together to help the long-term unemployed. More than 300 CEOs signed on to best practices for recruiting and hiring the long-term unemployed, including 80 of the nation's largest businesses and 20 from the Fortune 50. The President also required the Federal government to improve its hiring practices. The Administration is continuing to work with employers to learn and build on what works in helping the long-term unemployed return to steady jobs. Additionally, the Administration will use $150 million in existing funds to scale up partnerships between employers and non-profits that help get the long-term unemployed back to work through work-based training, job placement assistance, and employer outreach.

Second, take steps to raise wages and ensure that growth is broadly shared

A stronger economy will help raise wages, and, conversely, higher wages will help strengthen the economy. That is why it is essential to raise the minimum wage. While Congress has waited to act, many states and businesses are moving ahead. But the only way for approximately 28 million Americans to get a raise would be for Congress to give them one—a step that would also strengthen aggregate demand and provide a near-term boost to the economy.

Over the longer run, wages would also benefit from institutional arrangements that strengthened the leverage that workers have in wage negotiations, from increased education and skills, and from better matching to jobs.

Third, although the aging of the population will continue to slow labor-force growth, a range of measures could help offset this trend and expand potential growth.

The participation rate, of course, is not a goal unto itself. If more people retire solely because they are older and have saved and contributed for their full working lives, that can be a natural and beneficial development. But the declining participation rate also subtracts from potential economic growth and exacerbates our future fiscal challenges. Moreover, not all of the decline in participation we have seen is the result of natural and good developments—in fact the long-term trend of declining participation and employment rates for many groups is very troubling and clearly merits a policy response.

Part of the answer to these challenges is enabling older workers who want to continue to work to do so. Workplace flexibility policies that allow employees to work part-time or flexible hours can help older workers tailor their jobs to their specific needs and can create roles that are less demanding than full-time employment.

With women increasingly among our most skilled workers, boosting their participation is essential for strengthening growth. The President is working with employers and all levels of government to move forward on paid leave, greater workplace flexibility and other policies that can increase participation and productivity for both men and women. In line with that effort, he is pursuing legislative and executive actions to promote equal pay.

In addition, probably the most significant policy response to falling labor force participation rates is immigration reform, which would increase the size of the labor force and could raise the labor force participation rate. Immigrants tend to participate at higher rates than native-born Americans, partially due to the fact that they are younger on average. CBO estimates that the immigration reform bill passed by the Senate would add 6 million workers to the labor force by 2023, raising the participation rate by 0.7 percentage point.

Finally, building labor force attachment among young people can raise their labor force participation throughout life and offset the long-term declining trend. Earlier this year, the President announced $100 million in funding for American Apprenticeship Grants, which will use existing funds to expand apprenticeships, training young people for high-demand jobs and helping them build relationships with employers. Additionally, the Administration is awarding $500 million to community colleges to implement job training programs targeted to the skills and credentials demanded by businesses. The President has similarly committed to re-designing high school curricula to focus more on industry-relevant skills. All of these initiatives aim to give young people labor market skills and connect them with employment opportunities, raising their labor force participation over the long term.

Finally, employment for some groups, including prime age men and even more severely, young men of color, has been a long-standing challenge that was compounded by the recession.

As the economy has grown and transformed over the last sixty years, it has created rising wages and expanded opportunity for many. But some prime-age men have had challenges adjusting to the new patterns of employment, and as a result, the employment rate for prime-age men has fallen from 92 percent in 1950 to 83 percent today, as discussed above. This is one of the most significant long-standing challenges in the labor market and, unfortunately, one of the least understood. But we know some of the measures that would help, including the same steps that strengthen aggregate demand in the short run—like increasing our investments in infrastructure.

The situation for young black men is much more severe. This was not always the case. In 1950, the participation rate of young African-American men exceeded that of young white men. By 2014, this had reversed in dramatic fashion, with young white men participating at a rate of 59 percent. The comparable rate for young black men was just below half. In 1950, similar population shares of young black and white men were employed. Today the employment-to-population ratio for young white men is 52 percent, while for young African-American men it is 37 percent.

One of the most effective ways we can bring these groups into the labor force is by making work pay through the EITC. Research has consistently found that the EITC reduces poverty and increases employment—with previous EITC expansions bringing over half a million people into the labor force. That is why the President has proposed expanding the EITC for workers without children and for noncustodial parents to double its current value. This expansion would target groups with low labor force participation, including men without a college education, young adults not enrolled in school, and women without dependent children, greatly increasing incentives for all these groups to participate in the labor force.

To support young men of color, the President has launched the My Brother's Keeper initiative, which will determine the public and private efforts most effective at helping young men of color succeed, and help to bring these programs to scale. The initiative focuses heavily on remaining on-track in school, completing post-secondary education, entering the workforce, and staying out of the criminal justice system. Supporting young men of color throughout these life stages will help connect them with the labor force and ensure that they reach their full potential professionally. So far, eleven leading philanthropic foundations have committed to investing $200 million in this effort.

Conclusion

We now stand at 54 consecutive months of private-sector job growth and counting. The jobs that have comprised this progress have been overwhelmingly full-time, with their promise of restoring sound financial footing to millions of American households. And the unemployment rate has come down together with reductions in long-term unemployment, discouraged workers, marginally attached workers more broadly, and part-time jobs—representing a genuine improvement in labor utilization.

Yet major challenges remain. Even at a strong pace of recovery, the depth of the recession means that a full recovery will still take more time. And even after we are fully recovered, the job market will still face a number of challenges that have a meaningful structural dimension that pre-date the great recession, including long-term unemployment, people working part-time for economic reasons, the participation rate, and the degree of labor force churn.

Ultimately, for most Americans the biggest challenge they face is not finding a job but growing their wages. We have seen a falling unemployment rate translate into a pickup in wage growth, but it still does not match productivity growth—let alone come close to making up for decades of slower wage growth.

The good news is that we are making progress on all of these fronts. And they are complementary—steps to strengthen the economy, increase demand, and increase growth will ultimately translate into higher wages and incomes for American families. The key is continuing to move forward on these steps.

References

Aaronson, Stephanie, Bruce Fallick, Andrew Figura, Jonathan Pingle, and William Wascher. 2006. "The Recent Decline in the Labor Force Participation Rate and its Implications for Potential Labor Supply." Brookings Papers on Economic Activity.

Cajner, Tomaz and David Ratner. 2014. "The Recent Decline in the Long-Term Unemployment Rate." FEDS Notes.

(CBO) Congressional Budget Office. 2014. "The Slow Recovery of the Labor Market."

(CEA) Council of Economic Advisers. 2014. "The Labor Force Participation Rate Since 2007: Causes and Policy Implications" (July).

Davis, Steven J. and John Haltiwanger. 2014. "Labor Market Fluidity and Economic Performance." Jackson Hole Economic Symposium. Working Paper.

Elsby, Michael WL, Bart Hobijn, and Ayşegül Şahın. 2010. "The Labor Market in the Great Recession." Brookings Papers on Economic Activity.

Furman, Jason. 2014a. "Global Lessons for Inclusive Growth." The Institute of International and European Affairs. Dublin, Ireland. Speech.

Furman, Jason. 2014b. "Whatever Happened to the Great Moderation?" 23rd Annual Hyman P. Minksy Conference on the State of the U.S. and World Economics. The National Press Club, Washington, D.C. Speech.

Furman, Jason. 2014c. "America's Millenials in the Recovery." The Zillow Housing Forum. Washington, D.C. Speech.

Ghayad, Rand. 2014. "The Jobless Trap." Northeastern University. Dissertation Chapter.

Hyatt, Henry R. and James R. Spletzer. 2013. "The Recent Decline in Employment Dynamics." *IZA Journal of Labor Economics* 2, 5.

Jacobson, Louis S., Robert J. LaLonde, and Daniel G. Sullivan. 1993. "Earnings Losses of Displaced Workers." *The American Economic Review* 83, 4: 685-709.

Kahn, Matthew E. and David M. Levinson. 2011. "Fix It First, Expand It Second, Reward It Third: A New Strategy for America's Highways." The Hamilton Project, The Brookings Institution.

Kroft, Kory, Fabian Lange, Matthew Notowidigdo, and Lawrence Katz. 2014. "Long-term Unemployment and the Great Recession." *NBER Working Paper #20273*.

Krueger, Alan B., Judd Cramer and David Cho. 2014. "Are the Long-Term Unemployed on the Margins of the Labor Market?" Brookings Papers on Economic Activity.

Molloy, Raven, Christopher L. Smith, and Abigail Wozniak. 2013. "Declining Migration Within the U.S.: The Role of the Labor Market." NBER Working Paper 20065.

Oreopoulos, Philip, Marianne Page, and Ann Huff Stevens. 2008. "The Intergenerational Effects of Worker Displacement." *Journal of Labor Economics* 26, 3: 455-000.

Polivka, Anne E. and Stephen M. Miller. 1998. "The CPS After the Redesign: Refocusing the Lens." Chapter 7 in *Labor Statistics Measurement Issues*. University of Chicago Press.

Reinhart, Carmen M. and Vincent R. Reinhart. 2010. "After the Fall." Proceedings: Economic Policy Symposium. Federal Reserve Bank of Kansas City, Jackson Hole, KS: 17-60.

Sullivan, Daniel and Till Von Wachter. 2009. "Job Displacement and Mortality: An Analysis using Administrative Data." *The Quarterly Journal of Economics* 124, 3: 1265-1306.

White House. 2014. "Addressing the Negative Cycle of Long-Term Unemployment" (January).

ABSTRACT

This report addresses Generic Safety Issue (GSI) 188, "Steam Generator Tube Leaks or Ruptures Concurrent with Containment Bypass from Main Steam Line or Feedwater Line Breaches," which concerns the potential for additional tube leakage or ruptures from the growth of existing cracks in steam generator tubes resulting from the dynamic loads following a main steam line break (MSLB) or feedwater line break (FWLB). To address the issue, this report provides the technical findings from thermal-hydraulic transient analyses and sensitivity studies, a simplified finite-element model of steam generator support structures and tubes, and structural analyses and sensitivity studies of the potential for crack growth. The results show that the additional dynamic loads from an MSLB are greater than those from an FWLB. The report concludes that dynamic loads from an MSLB are low and do not affect the structural integrity of tubes and do not lead to additional leakage or ruptures beyond what would be determined using differential pressure loads alone. Therefore, GSI-188 is closed, and the staff recommends no changes to existing regulations or guidance with respect to the dynamic loads induced by a breach of the main steam or feedwater line.

FOREWORD

The work discussed in this report was performed to resolve a principal assertion of Generic Safety Issue (GSI) 188, "Steam Generator Tube Leaks or Ruptures Concurrent with Containment Bypass from Main Steam Line or Feedwater Line Breaches." Specifically, the principal assertion is that dynamic loads induced in steam generator tubes by a main steam line break (MSLB) or other secondary-side breaches would lead to growth of cracks and increased steam generator tube leakage or ruptures. The project required the use of thermal-hydraulics to evaluate pressure differentials on secondary-side steam generator structural components, as well as materials engineering to assess the integrity of the steam generator tubes. Staff from the U.S. Nuclear Regulatory Commission (NRC), Office of Nuclear Regulatory Research (RES), Division of Systems Analysis and Regulatory Effectiveness, Safety Margins and Systems Analysis Branch, performed the thermal-hydraulics work. The tube integrity analyses and research were conducted at Argonne National Laboratory (ANL), under the direction of the RES Division of Engineering Technology, Materials Engineering Branch.

The NRC initiated this work in response to a staff member's concern about the impact of an MSLB on the integrity of steam generator tubes. If an MSLB occurs, the difference in pressure between the primary coolant side of the steam generator tubes and the secondary side would increase because the secondary side would be depressurized. In addition, a steam line break may impose dynamic loads on the tube support plates (TSPs), and these loads could be transferred to the tubes. The effect of these additional dynamic loads on the integrity of degraded tubes during an MSLB formed the basis for the staff member's concern. Moreover, if the steam line break were to cause steam generator tubes to rupture, primary coolant (which contains radioactive particles) could be released to the atmosphere outside of the containment depending on the break location and plant design. A Generic Issues Review Panel reviewed the staff member's concern regarding steam line breaks and the possible effect on tube integrity and classified it as GSI-188.

The Safety Margins and Systems Analysis Branch conducted the thermal-hydraulics work using the TRAC-M computer code and hand calculations. The results yielded comparable estimates of pressure loading on the steam generator TSPs. The results were also comparable to those that Westinghouse obtained using its own computer code. The ANL staff then used the dynamic pressure loads from the thermal-hydraulics calculations to evaluate the stresses transferred to the steam generator tubes using finite-element analysis techniques. Vertical motion of the TSPs relative to the tubes as a result of the pressure pulse associated with an MSLB could transfer loads to the degraded tubes if they are locked to the TSP. If the degradation is great enough or the loads are high, existing cracks could propagate and lead to a possible leak or rupture of the tubes. By contrast, if enough tubes are locked to the TSPs, the loads on individual tubes would be low, and only very long throughwall circumferential cracks would propagate. Field experience, examinations, and tube pullout force results indicate that in steam generators experiencing significant degradation at the TSPs, a majority of the tubes are locked in place by corrosion or crevice deposits. The results of the integrity analyses that considered both the differential pressure stress and the dynamic loads show that if at least 40 tubes (out of several thousand) are locked in the TSPs, the additional dynamic loads associated with an MSLB would not cause any additional damage to the steam generator tubes because these loads were found to be insignificant.

Therefore, the staff concludes that the dynamic loads from an MSLB do not affect the structural integrity of tubes in service and do not lead to additional leakage or ruptures beyond what would be determined using differential pressure loads alone. Therefore, the principal assertion of GSI-188 is closed, and the staff recommends no changes to existing regulations or guidance with respect to the dynamic loads induced by a breach of the main steam or feedwater line.

Michael J. Case, Director
Division of Engineering
Office of Nuclear Regulatory Research
U.S. Nuclear Regulatory Commission

CONTENTS

EXECUTIVE SUMMARY

The U.S. Nuclear Regulatory Commission (NRC) developed Generic Safety Issue (GSI) 188, "Steam Generator Tube Leaks or Ruptures Concurrent with Containment Bypass from Main Steam Line or Feedwater Line Breaches," in response to a concern about the potential propagation of existing flaws produced by the additional loads resulting from resonance vibrations in steam generator tubes during steam line break depressurization. This is the principal area addressed in this resolution.

GSI-188 postulates that (1) a main steam or feedwater line break in an unisolable portion of the secondary system may cause multiple steam generator tubes to leak or rupture, or (2) significant steam generator tube leakage or rupture may cause an unisolable secondary-side breach that may, in turn, exacerbate the leakage. Either postulated accident scenario could have significant consequences because primary coolant could be lost to the environment through the leaking or ruptured steam generator tubes and the break in the secondary system.

This report describes the approach that the NRC staff used to resolve the principal assertion, the results of its studies, and the basis for closure. The NRC conducted the following studies:

- thermal-hydraulic (TH) transient analysis for temperature and pressure pulse loading during main steam line break (MSLB) and feedwater line break (FWLB) events

- analyses of the loads that are transferred to the steam generator tubes from the tube support plates (TSPs) during the transients of interest using a simplified (albeit conservative) finite-element model

- sensitivity integrity studies using the TH pressure drops to evaluate the failure of flawed steam generator tubes in a Westinghouse Model 51 steam generator during MSLB and FWLB events

- crack growth evaluations in the presence of vibrations in addition to the differential pressure stress

For new generators or generators where there is little degradation and the tubes are not locked, the TSPs are free to slide, and therefore, there is no mechanism to transfer the loads to the tubes. For generators where the tubes are locked in place, the level of loading that can be transferred to a degraded tube depends on the number of tubes that are locked (thereby distributing the loads) and the breakaway loads required to free the tubes from the TSP. The tube integrity evaluation used conservative breakaway loads.

Results show that the dynamic loads transferred to the steam generator tubes during an MSLB have virtually no effect on the burst pressure and leak-rate integrity of the tubes with axial cracks beyond the effects of differential pressure. The results also show that if some of the tubes in the steam generator are locked to the TSPs by corrosion products, the dynamic loads associated with an MSLB will have little impact on the integrity of the tubes unless extensive circumferential cracking is present. If only a few tubes are locked in each of the four quadrants, short throughwall circumferential cracks could propagate. When only 10 tubes per quadrant are locked, circumferential throughwall cracks must be longer than 180° in order to propagate. If all of the tubes are locked, the circumferential throughwall cracks must be longer than 300° for the cracks to grow under the influence of MSLB loads. These latter cracks would generally not be present in the steam generator during an MSLB, since inservice inspection or leakage would have revealed them, and plant personnel would have repaired or plugged them before the steam generator returned to normal operation. Field experience, examinations, and tube pullout force results indicate that in steam generators experiencing significant degradation at the TSPs, most of the tubes are locked in place so that the dynamic loads transferred to degraded tubes are low and large cracks can be tolerated.

The basis for closure of this generic safety issue is that the dynamic loads produced by an MSLB or FWLB would cause no additional damage to SG tubes containing flaws beyond the effect of differential pressure loads alone. As discussed above, tubes with large throughwall circumferential cracks that might have the potential to grow are not expected to be in service (i.e., they would have been plugged or sleeved before the circumferential extent became significant). The lateral load on the tubes is also greatest during an MSLB, but the loads are too low to cause significant bending stress in the tubes. In addition, the TH analysis demonstrates that the MSLB transient would show, at most, one or two significant load cycles and, therefore, fatigue caused by resonance vibrations is not an issue.

ACKNOWLEDGMENTS

The author gratefully acknowledges the contributions of Dr. Joseph Muscara of the U.S. Nuclear Regulatory Commission (NRC), Office of Nuclear Regulatory Research (RES), Division of Engineering (DE), for coordinating the RES efforts and for extensive review and comments. The author also acknowledges the contributions, review,and comments of Dr. Todd Mintz of RES. William J.Krotiuk in the RES Division of Systems Analysis and Regulatory Effectiveness, Safety Margins and Systems Analysis Branch, performed the thermal-hydraulics work. Dr. Saurin Majumdar, Dr. Ken Kasza, John Oats, Jeff Franklin, and Charles Vulyak, Jr., conducted the materials engineering work under the author's direction at Argonne National Laboratory. The Argonne National Laboratory program managers were Dr. William J. Shack and Dr. David S. Kupperman.

ABBREVIATIONS

ACRS	Advisory Committee on Reactor Safeguards (NRC)
ANL	Argonne National Laboratory
DE	Division of Engineering
EDM	electro-discharge machining
FWLB	feedwater line break
GSI	generic safety issue
ksi	kilopounds per square inch
kN	kilo-Newton
kPa	kilopascal
LOFT	loss-of-fluid test
lbf	pound-force
ME	Materials Engineering
MSLB	main steam line break
NRC	U.S. Nuclear Regulatory Commission
NRR	Office of Nuclear Reactor Regulation (NRC)
PRA	probabilistic risk assessment
PWR	pressurized-water reactor
psi	pounds per square inch
RES	Office of Nuclear Regulatory Research (NRC)
SG	steam generator
SGTR	steam generator tube rupture
SRP	Standard Review Plan
TH	thermal-hydraulic
TSP	tube support plate

1. INTRODUCTION

The U.S. Nuclear Regulatory Commission (NRC) developed Generic Safety Issue (GSI) 188, "Steam Generator Tube Leaks or Ruptures Concurrent with Containment Bypass from Main Steam Line or Feedwater Line Breaches," in response to a concern regarding resonance vibrations in steam generator (SG) tubes during steam line break depressurization. A member of the NRC staff believed that such vibrations could affect the validity of previous SG tube leak and rupture analyses (Ref. 1). This NRC staff member essentially postulated the following two potentially risk-significant events that are not fully addressed as design-basis accidents in final safety analysis reports, industry analyses, the NRC's Standard Review Plan (SRP) (Refs. 2 and 3),[1] or staff reviews:

(1)   Operating experience and design information suggest that the potential exists for a line breach to significantly increase SG leakage as a result of resonance vibration of SG tubes from a secondary-side blowdown.

(2)   Multiple SG tube leaks or ruptures could cause the secondary side to overpressurize and cause a steam line break that could then result in additional SG tube leaks or ruptures.

A letter from Nilesh Chokshi to Ashok C. Thadani, dated May 21, 2001 (Ref 4) describes the nature and scope of GSI-188. The objective of this report is to address the principal assertion of GSI-188. Specifically, this assertion is that the axial, bending, and cyclic loads induced in SG tubes from the shock wave and resonance vibrations resulting from a main steam line break (MSLB), or other secondary-side breaches, would lead to growth of cracks and increased SG tube leakage or ruptures outside the range of analyses and experiments done by the staff. A technical issue in GSI-188 related to calculations of the dynamic loads from an MSLB is that neither resonance vibrations nor cross-flow forces can be calculated by the one-dimensional RELAP thermal-hydraulic (TH) code that may have been previously used for similar evaluations. Another aspect of GSI-188 is its relationship to GSI-163, "Multiple Steam Generator Tube Leakage," since GSI-188 postulates a potential for multiple tube ruptures induced by the additional dynamic loads from an MSLB.

---

[1]   Applicable sections are 15.1.5, "Steam System Piping Failures Inside and Outside of Containment," and 15.6.3, "Radiological Consequences of Steam Generator Failure (PWR)." The reference list includes the draft update to the SRP (Ref. 3) because it documents and complies with regulatory requirements and staff positions that have been established elsewhere.

2. PLAN FOR RESOLUTION

The NRC used the following plan to resolve the principal assertion of GSI-188:

(1) Prepare a Task Action Plan to resolve GSI-188.

(2) Use information from existing analyses, as well as new results from the NRC Office of Nuclear Regulatory Research (RES) TH calculations and sensitivity studies during an MSLB, to estimate upper-bound loads (including cyclic loads) and displacements on SG tubes and tube support plates (TSPs) using the TRAC-M code. Factors to be considered include TSP and wrapper design; crevices that are packed, open, or mixed; TSP motion; and tube locking. Review other codes for more accurate predictions and potential use. Determine the effect of other secondary system breaks on tube performance. This could include the main feedwater line, the steam line supplying steam-driven auxiliary feedwater, or other steam supply lines. If substantial growth of existing degradation is observed when using upper-bound loads, calculate more realistic loads for the integrity analyses.

(3) Estimate crack growth, if any, for a range of crack types and sizes using bounding loads and displacements (or more realistic loads and displacements if deemed necessary) in addition to the pressure stresses, and include any effects from TSP movement and cyclic loads.

(4) Based on the potential for flaw growth, as determined in item 3 above, decide whether more refined TH analyses are required to more accurately identify the forces and displacements of structures under MSLB conditions.

(5) Test degraded tubes under pressure and with axial and bending loads, simulating the MSLB and other secondary-side depressurizing loads, to validate the analytical results.

(6) Conduct analyses (similar to those described above) with refined load estimates if necessary.

(7) Evaluate whether increased steam generator tube ruptures (SGTRs) or leaks could result in secondary-side breaches, which could further increase tube leakage as a result of resonance vibration within the affected SG tube bundle.

(8) Establish the impact of GSI-188 on GSI-163.

3

3. TECHNICAL FINDINGS

3.1 Thermal-Hydraulic Analyses

The TH analyses used in resolving GSI-188 are drawn from a report prepared by William J. Krotiuk, entitled "Analysis Report: Pressurized-Water Reactor Steam Generator Internal Loading Following a Main Steam or Feedwater Line Break," dated September 2002 (Ref. 5).

The Krotiuk study includes TH calculations and sensitivity studies using the TRAC-M computer code to assess the pressure loads on the TSPs and SG tubes during an MSLB or feedwater line break (FWLB). It also contains sensitivity studies on code and model parameters including solution methods. In addition, the study includes development of a conservative estimate of loads and an evaluation of that estimate against similar analyses. Krotiuk also performed a TH assessment of flow-induced vibrations during an MSLB. Using the TH conditions calculated during the transient, Krotiuk then generated a conservative estimate of flow-induced vibration displacement and frequency assuming steady-state behavior.

Specifically, the Krotiuk report provides the SG internal pressure loadings following an MSLB or FWLB, which can affect the structural integrity of the SG tubes. The pressure loadings developed through this analysis were then used in a structural assessment of SG tubes to determine the potential for flaw growth that might lead to increased tube leakage or ruptures. Toward that end, Krotiuk used the TRAC-M code to calculate upper-bound pressure loadings on the TSPs in a Westinghouse Model 51 SG. Specifically, the cases analyzed for this study include a guillotine MSLB near the SG nozzle, a flow restrictor-limited MSLB near the SG nozzle, and a guillotine FWLB near the SG nozzle. Krotiuk then compared the pressure loads calculated using the TRAC-M code against similar calculations contained in the Westinghouse "Model 51 Steam Generator Limited Tube Support Plate Displacement Analysis for Dented or Packed Tube to Tube Support Plate Crevices," dated August 1996 (Ref. 6). Additionally, Krotiuk compared the TRAC-M results against the results of a hand calculation performed using the Moody choked-flow method combined with calculations to follow the transport of the depressurization wave originating at the break location. In addition to the verification provided by comparing the results of the TRAC-M calculation with the Moody/acoustic hand calculation, Krotiuk also analyzed the Edwards Pipe Blowdown Experiment and the Loss-of-Fluid Test (LOFT) Semiscale Blowdown Test using the TRAC-M computer code. Results from the TRAC-M analysis of these two tests agree well with experimental measurements. Therefore, the staff concluded that the pressure loads calculated by Krotiuk are reliable.

The Krotiuk TRAC-M analysis, the Westinghouse analysis, and the Moody/acoustic hand calculation all conclude that a guillotine rupture of the steam line at hot standby conditions produces the largest pressure loadings on the TSPs. The peak loadings on the upper TSPs, calculated using TRAC-M, are close in value to those calculated using the Moody/acoustic method. The TRAC-M results are also close to the results of the TRANFLO and RELAP5 analysis presented in the Westinghouse report.

The Krotiuk report also presents calculated pressure loads on SG tubes at the bottom of the SG and at the SG tube bend following an MSLB. In addition, the report presents pressure differentials for the cylindrical shroud, which separates the primary boiling flow region around the SG tubes from the surrounding annular area through which feedwater flows. These additional pressure loads can directly or indirectly affect the integrity of the SG tubes. This is because the cylindrical shroud supports the TSPs, and, therefore, loads on the shroud may be transmitted to the SG tubes.

The Krotiuk TRAC-M analysis also indicates that the pressure loadings from an FWLB are substantially lower than those resulting from an MSLB. Therefore, an FWLB need not be further considered.

The assessment of the SG analyses using the TRAC-M computer code and the hand calculation using the Moody/acoustic method reveals that the primary loads are developed by the short-term TH and acoustic effects occurring in the first few seconds following the break. The study also indicates that flow-induced vibration loading, developed as the result of quasi-steady flow present after the completion of the short-term effects, produced smaller loads than the short-term loads. Consequently, a comprehensive long-term analysis was not performed.

Krotiuk recommended that a multiplier of 1.2 be applied to the results calculated using the TRAC-M model to account for the lack of a two-phase pressure drop multiplier for the irreversible form loss calculation in the current version of TRAC-M. The pressure loadings calculated using the TRAC-M code were used in a structural assessment of the SG tubes to determine whether those loadings, in addition to the differential pressure loading, contribute significantly to the growth of existing cracks.

3.2 Estimates of Upper-Bound Loads and Tube Integrity Analyses and Tests

Under contract to the NRC, Argonne National Laboratory (ANL) conducted sensitivity studies concerning the failure of flawed SG tubes using the Westinghouse Model 51 SG during an MSLB or FWLB (Ref. 7). As previously stated, the most critical transient (from the standpoint of SG tube integrity) is an MSLB from hot standby conditions. Such an event causes the highest pressure drops across the TSPs. The lateral pressure drop across individual tubes is also highest during an MSLB, but those loads are too low to cause significant bending stress (<1 ksi) in the SG tubes. The TH analysis also shows that the periods of fundamental vibration modes of the SG tubes and TSPs are sufficiently short, when compared with the rise time of the pressure pulse during the MSLB, so the inertia effects can be ignored and resonant vibration of the tubes should not be an issue (Ref. 7).

Static-elastic finite-element analyses of a Model 51 SG TSP, including the supports with and without a single tube locked to the TSP, show that the maximum TSP displacement under a unit pressure loading is reduced from 1.12 cm (0.44 in.) with no locked tubes to 0.137 cm (0.054 in.) with one locked tube. Thus, very little if any movement of the TSP is expected when a small percentage of the tubes is locked in the TSP. These displacements are consistent with industry findings (Ref. 6).

To assess "worst-case" scenarios, in which only a small number of tubes are locked, ANL developed a simplified (albeit conservative) finite-element model of the seven TSPs of a Model 51 SG, including the supporting stay rods and wedges. In that model, the stay rods and wedges are assumed to provide rigid support to the TSPs. Interaction between the TSPs was modeled by the locked SG tubes only. The tubes were assumed to be fixed to the tubesheet, which was assumed to be rigid. Approximate analyses were carried out with 1, 2, 4, and 10 tubes in each quadrant locked to the TSPs. The location of the locked tubes was selected conservatively to be at the point of maximum transverse displacement of the TSP when the tubes are freely sliding within the TSPs. Unit pressure drop (upward) analyses for each TSP show that the pressure load was primarily transferred as tensile axial load on the locked SG tube sections below the loaded TSP, although about 10 to 15 percent of the load was carried as axial compressive load in the tube section above the loaded TSP. As expected, the axial load per tube steadily decreased as the number of locked tubes increased. The analyses show that the bending stresses in the tube from TSP movement are low because the axial stiffness of the SG tubes is far greater than the bending stiffness of the TSPs, which is significantly reduced by the numerous tube holes and flow holes. Thus, the direct axial stress is the controlling factor for tube integrity. Since the stiffness of the newer TSP designs (trefoil, quatrefoil) is expected to be similar to the drill-holed TSPs, the results from these studies are applicable to the newer designs.

ANL used the results of the unit pressure drop analysis to calculate the axial loads that act on the various tube sections of the Model 51 SG under an MSLB transient pressure-drop loading on the TSPs. The ANL analysis used the TRAC-M pressure drops multiplied by an uncertainty factor of 1.5. This is conservative when compared to the factor of 1.2 recommended by Krotiuk. In the case where only a few tubes are assumed to be locked, initial analysis results show that unrealistically large loads were transferred from the TSPs to the locked SG tubes with the conservative assumption that the tubes were completely locked to the TSP under all loads. Loads will not be transferred to the tubes beyond the tube pullout load because the tube is released from the support plate. A review of tube pullout data from a retired SG from a foreign plant with drilled-hole carbon steel TSPs shows that the mean value of the tube pullout load at operating temperature was 2700 lbf (12 kN) per tube per intersection, and a reasonable upper bound (95-percent confidence limit) is 4000 lbf (18 kN) per tube per intersection, which was used for most of the tube integrity analyses. ANL also reviewed data for tubes pulled through four TSP intersections and part of the tubesheet (top 4 in.; the rest of the tubesheet-to-tube interfacial bond was removed by flame cutting before the tube pull) from a domestic nuclear power plant, which was removed from service (Table 1). Distributing the total pullout force equally among the five intersections, the mean pullout force at room temperature per intersection is 2725 lbf (12.12 kN), which is comparable to the mean pullout force of 3120 lbf (13.88 kN) for the foreign plant. (Note that this value corresponds to 2700 lbs at operating temperature, as previously discussed.) The staff recently received data from additional U.S. plants, and all of these pullout forces are consistent. The loads that can be transferred to the tube depend on the breakaway load (pullout load). The TSP design and material, tube material, environment, age of plant, and level of degradation all affect the breakaway loads. Newer plants with lower operating times and newer materials and designs (trefoil and quatrefoil) are expected to have either freely sliding TSPs or lower pullout forces than the TSPs described above. Since the 4000-lbf (18-kN) load used in this study is conservative for degraded plants, it is even more conservative for newer plants to which the results would also apply.

Even when the maximum tube pullout force is limited to more realistic values, the calculated axial tensile stresses on the locked tubes at lower elevations are close to the ultimate tensile strength if only one or two tubes are assumed to be locked at the TSPs. This alone would not suggest rupture of the locked tube if it was unflawed, because large plastic displacement of the tube would be required, and that cannot occur in the SG. However, this does imply that the tolerance for circumferential cracks in these tubes would be severely limited. It is highly improbable that only one or two tubes out of more than 3000 tubes in the SG that is experiencing degradation could be locked to the TSPs while the rest are free to slide. A more plausible assumption is that multiple tubes (at least 10 per quadrant) are locked to the TSPs. The analyses shows that if 10 neighboring tubes in a quadrant are locked to each TSP, the maximum axial load in the locked tubes is significantly reduced, and the maximum throughwall stable circumferential crack length in the tubes at all of the TSP junctions is 180°. If all of the tubes are locked, the stable throughwall crack length is 300°. The results also show that the dynamic loads transferred to the SG tubes during the transients have virtually no effect on the burst pressure and leak-rate integrity of the tubes with axial cracks, beyond the effects of differential pressure only. Therefore, the dynamic loads from an MSLB do not affect the structural integrity of the tubes with either axial or circumferential cracks and do not lead to additional leakage or ruptures in current or replacement SGs.

Although the TH results for the MSLB transient show at most one or two pressure pulse peaks, ANL conducted fatigue analyses to demonstrate that sufficient margin would exist for crack growth if the pressure-drop pulses occur repeatedly. The cyclic crack growth rate analyses show that the average growth rate for throughwall circumferential cracks just before rupture is on the order of only 0.1°/cycle. With as few as 16 tubes locked (4 tubes per quadrant), circumferential throughwall cracks that are less than or equal to 85° in extent would not grow to failure. Similarly, with 40 tubes locked (10 tubes per quadrant), cracks that are less than or equal to 230° in extent would not grow to failure. In addition, if the cracks are only partially throughwall, even longer cracks can be tolerated. The analyses were conducted using approximately 75 cycles at the peak load. As previously discussed and based on the TH results, an MSLB produces only one to two pressure pulse peaks. Therefore, no crack growth is expected under an MSLB attributable to resonant vibrations.

Table 1 Summary of Tube Pullout Force Data from the Domestic Plant Across Four TSPs and Partial (top 4 in.) Tubesheet Intersections

Tube Number	Breakaway Pressure (psi/kPa)	Multiplier (in.^{2}/cm^2)	Force (lbf/kN)	Force per Intersection (lbf/kN)
R14 C55	2100/14500	3.534/21.6	7421/33.01	1484/6.6
R5 C17	3500/24100	4.472/28.9	15652/69.62	3130/13.9
R45 C540	3800/26200	3.534/21.6	13429/59.73	2685/11.9
R5 C51	2000/13790	3.534/21.6	7068/31.44	1413/6.2
R7 C24	4400/30340	4.472/28.9	19677/87.52	3935/17.5
R4 C43	3000/20690	3.534/21.6	10602/47.16	2120.4/9.4
R17 C90	4800/33100	4.472/28.9	21466/95.48	4293/19.0
R39 C57	2800/19310	4.472/28.9	12522/55.83	2504/11.1
R5 C4	3200/22060	4.472/28.9	14310/63.65	2862/12.7
R13 C89	3000/20690	4.472/28.9	13416/59.67	2683/11.9
R33 C33	3200/22060	4.472/28.9	14310/63.65	2862/12.7
Mean per Intersection				2725/12.1

To confirm results from the tube integrity analyses, burst tests were conducted on 36-in. long Alloy 600TT SG tubes with 1-in. long axial electro-discharge machining (EDM) notches and 240°, 270°, and 300° circumferential EDM notches at the clamped end and the other end simply supported. Various transverse loads were then hung at the midsection to produce bending loads. The results of burst tests show that the transverse load had a significantly more pronounced effect on the burst pressure of specimens with circumferential EDM notches than on those with axial EDM notches. For the part-throughwall axial notch, the ligament rupture pressure increased slightly with increasing transverse load. By contrast, the burst pressure of tubes containing a throughwall axial notch was relatively insensitive to the transverse load. In addition, for specimens with a throughwall circumferential notch, the maximum notch opening displacement decreased and the burst pressure increased with decreasing transverse load. As previously discussed, the bending loads from TSP movement are negligible compared to direct axial loads from TSP movement and will not significantly affect the burst pressure under MSLB conditions. These tests validated model predictions for burst pressure and crack opening as a function of transverse loads.

As previously noted, industry calculations using RELAP5 and NRC staff calculations using the TRAC-M code yield comparable results for pressure drops across the TSPs as a result of an MSLB. In addition, both the industry and the NRC staff have undertaken bounding analyses of the pressure drops that yielded comparable results. Use of these conservative pressure drops from the TH results in tube integrity analyses shows that the dynamic loads had little effect on the propagation of existing flaws. Thus, there is no need for additional TH analysis to better define the loads for integrity evaluations.

3.3 Increased SGTRs or Leaks Inducing Secondary-Side Breaches

GSI-188 asserts that multiple SG tube leaks or ruptures could cause the secondary side to overpressurize and cause a steam line break that could then result in additional SG tube leaks or ruptures. In the event of a significant SGTR or leak, the reactor would scram and the operators would have to identify the source of the leak. The secondary-side radiation alarms would be activated, alerting the operators that an SG is the source of the leak. If the operators act quickly, they can identify which generator is leaking; however, if they wait, the contaminated water will reach the condenser, and all of the SGs will have contaminated water on the secondary side from the auxiliary feedwater system. The immediate operator action is to reduce the primary pressure to a value below the secondary-side pressure to stop the leaking of contaminated water out of the primary system. This is accomplished by isolating the SG with the leaking tube(s) and opening the steam dump valves on the nonleaking SGs.

The maximum pressure that the secondary side can experience is determined by the setpoints on the secondary-side safety relief valves, which are normally set a small percentage above normal operating pressures. Because the components are designed with much larger margins, no secondary-side breaches are expected.

4. SUMMARY, CONCLUSIONS, AND CLOSURE

This report describes the approach that the NRC staff used to resolve the principal assertion of GSI-188 and associated issues and provides the basis for closure. Specifically, the principal assertion is that the axial, bending, and cyclic loads induced in SG tubes by the additional dynamic loading from an MSLB or other secondary-side breaches would lead to growth of cracks and increased SG tube leakage or ruptures beyond the effects of differential pressure stress alone. Also, a proposed scenario suggested that multiple SG tube leaks or ruptures could cause the secondary side to overpressurize and cause a steam line break that could then result in additional SG tube leaks or ruptures.

To address the structural integrity of degraded tubes under the dynamic loads of an MSLB or other secondary-side breaches, TH evaluations of the pressure loads were conducted and used in structural analyses. In his TH work, Krotiuk estimated conservative values of differential pressures on the TSPs by using the TRAC-M computer code and Moody/acoustic hand calculations. These two evaluations produced similar results. Krotiuk's results were also similar to results from Westinghouse analyses using TRANFLO and RELAP5. The TRAC-M code was successfully benchmarked by analyzing the Edwards Pipe Blowdown Experiment and the LOFT Semiscale Blowdown Test. Therefore, the staff concluded that the conservative pressure loads calculated by Krotiuk are reliable, and those loads were used for the integrity analyses. The TH calculations determined that of all secondary-side breaches, the MSLB produced the highest pressure loads.

The structural analyses of tube integrity conducted at ANL using the conservatively adjusted Krotiuk results for MSLB show that bending loads transmitted to the tubes from TSP movement were low. Therefore, these loads will have minimal effect on the structural integrity of the tubes. The results also show that when 1 to 2 percent of the tubes are locked in the TSPs, the axial loading imposed on the SG tubes from MSLB dynamic loads does not significantly affect the structural integrity of even severely degraded tubes. Consequently, the staff concluded that dynamic loads from an MSLB will not affect the structural integrity of tubes in service and will not lead to additional leakage or ruptures beyond what would be determined using differential pressure alone. Therefore, the principal assertion of GSI-188 is not substantiated, and the issue is closed.

The staff also evaluated the contention that multiple SG tube leaks or ruptures could lead to additional secondary-side breaches. This evaluation led the staff to conclude that because the secondary-side pressures cannot exceed the relatively low pressure of the relief valve setpoints, there is virtually no potential for failures based on design margins. Therefore, the principal assertion is not substantiated, and the issue is closed.

The results of the structural tube integrity evaluations from Reference 7 show that the dynamic loads from an MSLB or FWLB will not significantly affect tube failure or leakage. Thus, these dynamic loads need not be considered in evaluating the potential for multiple tube ruptures under GSI-163.

The staff met with the NRC's Advisory Committee on Reactor Safeguards (ACRS), Subcommittees on Materials and Metallurgy and Thermal-Hydraulics, on February 3–4, 2004, and with the main Committee on February 5, 2004, to discuss progress on tasks in the Steam Generator Action Plan, which include Task 3.1 related to the principal assertion of GSI-188. The staff presented the technical basis for resolution of the principal assertion related to effects of dynamic loads on tube integrity during an MSLB. In a letter, dated May 21, 2004, to W.D. Travers (the NRC's Executive Director for Operations at that time), the ACRS agreed that "the analyses of the effects of depressurization during an MSLB on tube integrity have been completed, and item 3.1 is appropriately closed out" (Ref. 8). Therefore, the ACRS supports the closeout of the principal assertion of GSI-188.

5. REFERENCES

1. Memorandum from R. Spence to J.T. Wiggins and I. Canton, "Resonance Vibrations in Steam Generator Tubes During Steam Line Break Depressurization" (ADAMS Accession No. ML003726252), U.S. Nuclear Regulatory Commission, Washington, DC, May 22, 2000.

2. NUREG-0800, "Standard Review Plan for the Review of Safety Analysis Reports for Nuclear Power Plants" (ADAMS Accession No. ML033580033), U.S. Nuclear Regulatory Commission, Washington, DC, July 1981.

3. NUREG-0800, "Standard Review Plan for the Review of Safety Analysis Reports for Nuclear Power Plants" (ADAMS Accession No. ML033580677), Draft Report for Comment, U.S. Nuclear Regulatory Commission, Washington, DC, June 1996.

4. Memorandum from N. Chokshi to A.C. Thadani, Director, Office of Nuclear Regulatory Research, "Initial Screening of Candidate Generic Issue 188, 'Steam Generator Tube Leaks or Ruptures, Concurrent with Containment Bypass from Main Steam Line or Feedwater Line Breaches'" (ADAMS Accession No. ML011410572), U.S. Nuclear Regulatory Commission, Washington, DC, May 21, 2001.

5. Krotiuk, W.J., "Pressurized-Water Reactor Steam Generator Internal Loading Following a Main Steam or Feedwater Line Break" (ADAMS Accession No. ML023650122), SMSAB-02-05, U.S. Nuclear Regulatory Commission, Washington, DC, September 2002.

6. WCAP-14707, "Model 51 Steam Generator Limited Tube Support Plate Displacement Analysis for Dented or Packed Tube to Tube Support Plate Crevices," Westinghouse Electric Company, Pittsburgh, PA, August 1996.

7. Majumdar, S, et al. (Argonne National Laboratory), "Sensitivity Studies of Failure of Steam Generator Tubes During Main Steam Line Break and Other Secondary Side Depressurization Events," May 2007.

8. Letter from M.V. Bonaca to W.D. Travers, Executive Director for Operations, "Resolution of Certain Items Identified by the ACRS in NUREG-1740, 'Voltage-Based Alternative Repair Criteria' (ADAMS Accession No. ML041450305), U.S. Nuclear Regulatory Commission, Washington, DC, May 21, 2004.